You Can Double Your Class

2
AX

in Two Years or Less

By Josh Hunt

Group

Loveland, Colorado

Special thanks to Gary Aschbacher, Kevin Pyle, Jim Wilson,
Barry McCarty, Charlie Bass, Paul Stith, Ed Jent, and Dan
Orth for helpful editorial comments.

You Can Double Your Class in Two Years or Less

Copyright © 1997 Josh Hunt

Visit our Web site: **www.group.com**

Credits
Editor: Bob Buller
Managing Editor: Michael D. Warden
Chief Creative Officer: Joani Schultz
Copy Editor: Candace McMahan
Art Director: Jean Bruns
Cover Art Director: Helen H. Lannis
Designer: Randy Kady
Computer Graphic Artist: Kari K. Monson
Cover Designer: Richard Martin
Production Manager: Gingar Kunkel

Unless otherwise noted, Scriptures taken from the HOLY BIBLE, NEW INTER-
NATIONAL VERSION®. Copyright © 1973, 1978, 1984 by International Bible
Society. Used by permission of Zondervan Publishing House. All rights reserved.

Library of Congress Cataloging-in-Publication Data
Hunt, Josh.
    You can double your class in two years or less / by Josh Hunt.
      p.   cm.
    Includes bibliographical references.
    ISBN 0-7644-2019-4
    1. Christian education of adults. 2. Church growth. I. Title.
  BV1488.H87 1997
  268'.434--dc21   96-48998
                                                                  CIP

18   08 07
Printed in the United States of America.

CONTENTS

Section One:
The Vision!

Section Two:
The Means—TIGER!

Teach a halfway decent lesson each and every week—nothing less will do.

Invite every member and every prospect to every fellowship every month.

Section Three:
Getting the Job Done

It all begins with prayer.

It is my prayer that sometime while you are reading this book you will have a *eureka!* experience: "Hey, I can do this, and it does matter; in fact, nothing could matter more!" Before you go out and buy a tent to conduct your own crusade, however, I suggest that you take a few minutes to write down what you're feeling. You may want to use the space below to write a prayer to God.

_____

_____

_____

_____

_____

_____

_____

_____

_____

_____

_____

_____

_____

_____

_____

_____

_____

_____

_____

_____

Section One:
The Vision!

I invite you to embrace the vision of a better world made possible by a church that is making a difference in the world. I invite you to become part of an army of believers who are using their gifts to grow their groups and to double their classes every two years or less.

A Worthy Goal

We *can* reach our nation for Christ.

We can transform America with an army of small-group leaders like you who have a vision for doubling their classes every two years or less. We can do it because we can do all things through Christ, who strengthens us. We can be obedient to what God told us to do. I want to do that, don't you?

Think of it. There are approximately 320,000 Protestant and Catholic churches in America.[1] My experience has shown that each one probably has an average attendance of seventy-five and about seven Sunday school classes. That means that on any given weekend there are approximately twenty-four million people attending church and more than two million people teaching Sunday school. Suppose half or a fourth or even a tenth of the Sunday school teachers in America committed to doubling their class ten times during the next twenty years. Suppose we had only twenty-five thousand teachers from various denominations and churches on board. If each one doubled every two years or less, we would reach America in a little more than twenty years.[2]

Years	Teachers	Students
	25,000	250,000
2	50,000	500,000
4	100,000	1,000,000
6	200,000	2,000,000
8	400,000	4,000,000
10	800,000	8,000,000
12	1,600,000	16,000,000
14	3,200,000	32,000,000
16	6,400,000	64,000,000
18	12,800,000	128,000,000
20	25,600,000	256,000,000

I think God would be pleased if we did that. But it would be nothing special. We would only be doing what God has told us to do. In Luke 17:10 Jesus reminds us: "So you also, when you have done everything you were told to do, should say, 'We are unworthy servants; we have only done our duty.' "

Giving the ministry to people who are using their gifts to grow their groups will get the job done. In addition, it is a way to obey the Great Commission (Matthew 28:19-20) and to follow God's bread-and-butter strategy for spreading the gospel to all the world.

We often undertake big projects in our churches. We sponsor programs, musicals, and mission trips. We build big buildings, sponsor special conferences, and orchestrate spectacular Easter celebrations.

When we do these things, it's easy to lose sight of the importance of the basics. We are mesmerized by the sight of the home run sailing over the fence and forget the basics such as the routine ground ball. Small-group work is to church work what the routine ground ball is to baseball. It is the place where the work of the church happens. Most of what it means to be a church happens best in small groups. Teaching, caring, sharing, reaching, loving, encouraging, and helping happen best in, through, and around small groups. All the other ministries are good, but we should never lose our focus on the basics.

We may support all kinds of supplemental programs to help us grow, but it is the work of the small-group leader that lays the foundation for long-term growth. Consistently and quietly growing, reaching, teaching, assimilating, and doing what God tells us to do—this is the bread and butter of our ongoing strategy.

If the goal of reaching America in twenty years is a little hard for you to wrap your brain around, personalize it to your church or denomination. Southern Baptists, for example, have approximately four million people attending Sunday school each week. If half of the Southern Baptist classes doubled every two years or less, they alone would reach America with the gospel in less than twenty years.

Think about your own church. If you have one hundred people attending right now, you would reach in excess of three thousand people in ten years. One hundred to over three thousand in ten years is exciting. How many people would you reach if each group doubled every two years or less? Fill in the following chart to find out.

	Example	Your Church
Current attendance	100	
2 years	200	
4 years	400	
6 years	800	
8 years	1,600	
10 years	3,200	

Growing from one hundred to over three thousand in ten years is hard to fathom, but that's not the most exciting part. That's reserved for the second ten years. Even if only half the groups in your Sunday school were successful, you would still experience phenomenal growth. Go ahead, play with the math if you're given to that kind of thing.

Doubling your class every two years is a worthy goal. It will result in phenomenal growth. It will begin to help us obey the Great Commission.

Small groups are God's way to make disciples.

There is another reason why this is a worthy goal. There is no disciple-making without small groups.[3] God's plan for forming spiritually mature disciples involves getting them in groups (John 13:34-35; Hebrews 10:23-35). People do not climb Mount Everest alone. But every year, little groups, little platoons, little bands of friends, scale its lofty heights.

In the same way, people do not reach spiritual maturity alone. But in groups, among friends they can reach maturity and have fun while they do it. It won't always be easy, but it can be fun.

Let me explain what I mean. Vietnam veteran William Broyles writes in his book, *Brothers in Arms*:

> A part of me loved war. Now, please understand, I'm a peaceful man, fond of children and animals. And I believe that war should have no place in the

affairs of men. But the comradeship our platoon experienced in that war provides an enduring and moving memory in me. A comrade in war is someone you can trust with anything because you regularly trust him with your life. In war, individual possessions and advantage count for nothing. The group, the unit, the platoon is everything.[4]

> "A part of me loved war." William Broyles

Broyles goes on to describe how platoon members shared rice rations and passed around single cigarettes and shared the use of bamboo cots. He writes, "In war, we regularly risked our lives to recover our wounded and dead. We often felt close enough to each other to call one another brothers." Then, after describing the depth of feeling among the platoon members, he says once again: "A part of me loved war."

Why is Broyles so passionate about his feelings, his *positive* feelings for Vietnam? I thought we all hated Vietnam. I contend that it is because of the little-platoon experience, the experience of sharing one's life with others. And this little-platoon experience is basic to Christian discipleship. People long for it; they need it. There is no maturity without it.

There is an epidemic of loneliness in America. People long for love. They long for the love that only the church can give. God has commanded us to love them, and the quickest way for us to reach people for Christ is by loving them through small-group ministries. If we love them, they will come.

We can reach America through small groups that double every two years or less. We can make disciples in small groups that grow and double every two years. We cannot do it just with the professional clergy. Granted, we need these professionals. I'm not against

> If we love them, they will come.

professionals—I am one—but we cannot depend on professionals alone to get the job done. The job is simply too big. We must turn the work over to the people of God. This is the way God designed it in the first place.

Doubling your class is a worthy goal. Worthy of you giving your life to. We can change the face of Christianity in our generation. And the bread and butter of our strategy is the person doing the work in the trenches: you, the small-group leader. So let's get to the work.

NOTES

[1] George Barna, *Evangelism That Works* (Ventura, CA: Regal Books, 1995), 23.

[2] Before you get the wrong idea, let me assure you that "doubling your class" is not primarily a matter of increasing your attendance or building impressive numbers. It's about befriending and loving people outside of your church or group, introducing them to Jesus, and making them a part of your group and of your life. It's a matter of inviting people to become committed disciples of Jesus Christ.

[3] I use the terms Sunday school, small group, and small-group Bible study interchangeably because the principles I discuss in this book apply to all of them.

[4] William Broyles Jr., *Brothers in Arms* (New York, NY: Avon Books, 1987), quoted by Bill Hybels in the sermon "Enlisting in Little Platoons."

An Attainable Goal

If doubling our classes every two years or less is all that is needed to reach our generation with the gospel, our goal must be lofty, unattainable, and unrealistic.

Wrong.

It's tempting to think that this goal is too big for us, that it is beyond our grasp. In fact, after reading the first chapter, that's probably what you are thinking right now. It sounds like lofty idealism. But if I communicate well in this chapter, you will not think that much longer!

You *can* double your class in two years or less. I want to show you how.

The question is, how fast does a class have to grow in order to double in two years? We need some benchmarks along the way to evaluate our progress. The short answer is 40 percent annual growth. Let me explain.

Church-growth experts look at growth in a special way. They are fond of talking about percentage growth, specifically, about annual percentage growth. They call this the annual growth rate. It is computed by dividing the amount of growth by the original amount of attendance. For example, if a class is averaging ten and grows by four to produce a new average of fourteen, the formula works like this:

4 ÷ 10 = .4 or 40% growth

I used this example on purpose because this is exactly what the average class needs to do to double in two years. Doubling every two years works out to about a 40 percent annual growth rate. In my experience, the average class has about ten people present each Sunday. Some have more, some a little less, but the average is about ten. Let's assume your class has about ten in attendance each week. In order to double in two years, you will need to average fourteen by the end of the first year. This means that each quarter during the first year you will need to pick up one person. *One person per quarter!* That is an attainable goal. But, as I pointed out earlier, if every class would do this, it would result in phenomenal growth. It would result in the fulfilling of the Great Commission. I believe the Father would be pleased by that.

What about the next year? Same thing: 40 percent growth. Only now you have fourteen people attending class, and 40 percent growth means adding one new person every two months instead of one every three months. This is growth so gradual you will need a micrometer to measure it.

Growing by one every other month the second year should be just as easy as increasing by one per quarter the first year. This is because you will have a bigger group to work with. A bigger group means more workers and more contacts with outsiders. Research has shown that the average person in a Sunday school class has five good contacts with outsiders. This means that when you grow from ten to fourteen you increase the number of contacts with outsiders by twenty. You also have four more people who can give Friday nights to Jesus (more on this later), plan fellowships, invite prospects, and so on.

I actually challenge groups to a slightly higher goal than this because most of us don't get around to doing everything we would like to do. So I build in a fudge factor in my goals. Here is the goal with the fudge factor: You need to thoroughly assimilate one new couple or two new people every quarter. Assimilate two people per quarter—that's all we need to do to reach America for Christ.

> *A person is thoroughly assimilated when his or her name is scribbled on the back of half a dozen phone books.*

Now let me give you a practical definition of assimilation. A person is thoroughly assimilated when his or her name is scribbled on the back of half a dozen phone books. That person is loved and included. That person is well on the way to becoming a disciple. People who know a lot of Bible facts but who are not loved and included, on the other hand, are prime candidates for inactive status. They are not on the path of discipleship; they are on their way out of the church. One survey reports that 75 percent of church dropouts said they left their churches because they didn't feel anyone cared whether they were there or not.[1] Here is the remedy for that: Thoroughly assimilate one couple or two people every quarter.

Let me clarify what I'm saying. First, I am talking about the average class of ten. If you are already averaging twenty, then, of course, you would need to assimilate two couples per quarter. (You also need to start a new group. You are quickly losing your status as a *small* group.)

Second, I am talking about actual attendance, not about enrollment. In churches that use class rosters, average attendance is normally about

50% of the average enrollment. If you do a good job of building relationships within the group, you can increase the percentage to above 50 percent, sometimes as high as 75 percent or better. Be careful, however. The point is not to increase the percentage. The goal is to reach people. If you are concerned only with percentages, why not just delete from your roster everyone who does not attend regularly? That will instantly increase your percentage. Of course, those folks may be offended that you deleted them, but your class will *look* more successful. If, on the other hand, you leave these sporadic attendees on the roster, you will be more likely to invite them to monthly fellowships, which is likely to get them back on the track of discipleship.

Finally, note that I am talking about net gain. You will always experience some attrition. Some will move away or become inactive. Normally, attrition is about 5 to 10 percent per year. In other words, a church has to attract 5 to 10 percent of its current attendance in new members just to stay even. A class of ten will need to attract one new member every year just to stay at ten. Still, a net gain of two new people each quarter is an attainable goal.

Summary

If you want to double your class every two years or less and you are currently averaging ten, you will need to add one person each quarter during the first year. (You'll also need to replace people who move away or become inactive.) If you do this, you will be well on your way to doubling in two years or less. To help you do this, set a goal of reaching and assimilating two people or one couple per quarter. The way to begin is to take responsibility for the task, which is the subject of the next chapter.

NOTES

[1] Rick Warren, *The Purpose Driven Church* (Grand Rapids, MI: Zondervan, 1995), 324.

Who Owns This Class, Anyway?

If *they* would get us a better room...
If *they* would just be more faithful...
If *they* would just all show up on the same Sunday...
If *they* would just get me more prospects...
If *they* were better organized...
If this literature were...
If the pastor...
If the...
If...

It is easier to make excuses than it is to make things happen. But it is infinitely more fun to make things happen. It is fun being a spectator, infinitely more fun being a player.

They don't erect statues to people who make articulate and erudite excuses. But there are statues all over the world erected to people who made things happen. In addition, God will pass out the rewards to the ones who made things happen. Ephesians 6:8 reminds us, "...you know that the Lord will reward everyone for whatever good he does."

Our reward in heaven will not be based on how well we blamed others for not getting things done. Neither will it be based on faith or grace. Salvation is about faith and grace. Rewards are about what we do. Jesus explains, "For the Son of Man is going to come in his Father's glory with his angels, and then he will reward each person *according to what he has done*" (Matthew 16:27, emphasis added).

What I want to impress on you in this chapter is very simple: God will hold us responsible for getting done what he wants us to get done. If you need a better room, do what you can to get one. In all likelihood, you can have a better room if you ask. Your pastoral team is there to make you successful in your ministry. They probably want to help you be successful. But let us never get confused about where the responsibility lies.

God has given you responsibility for your class. It's your baby. If it is your baby, you have to feed it. I believe in the autonomy of the local small group. You and your group members are ultimately responsible for the health and growth of the group. Pastors are there to make you successful in your ministry, but you are responsible to do what God wants you to do, to go where God leads you.

> *I believe in the autonomy of the local small group.*

With responsibility comes authority. If you are responsible, you get to make the decisions. You get to decide on the specifics of the goals and on the organization of the group. I am going to outline in this book a plan that will work. But I want you to feel free to alter the plan in any way that works for you. You and your group members get to make the decisions for your group.

For example, I advise my teachers to select their own literature if they choose. I have my preferences, but it is their preference that matters. I have found that teachers are far more motivated to teach what they want to teach than they are to teach what I want them to teach. In addition, each group can choose its target audience. Its members can invite whomever they want. I encourage free, open competition for visitors. First come, first served. People have argued with me about this: "They shouldn't be inviting them—they are *our* prospects." Then invite them; two invitations won't hurt. Let the person decide which class to attend after two friendly invitations. This is far better than no invitations at all. Anyone can invite anyone to come to class. If the high school students want to invite little old ladies, they can invite little old ladies.

I have also been asked, "What if visitors receive calls from more than one class inviting them to join?" Friend, that is not our problem. Our problem is that visitors by the bushelbasket are being ignored and neglected.

How far do we press this idea of giving ownership of the class to the teacher and the class members? What if a teacher promotes ideas that aren't biblical? What if the teacher begins presenting the Book of Mormon as truth? In those cases we must get out of our chairs, walk down the hall, and say, "Not in our church, not in our name." I ask teachers to let me know what they're teaching, and word gets around. If I heard something that I thought was unbiblical, I would ask the teacher to teach something else. But, in all honesty, it has never happened to me. I have not found people nearly as

> *Pastors are there to make you successful in your ministry.*

fascinated by heresy as we might think. God's plan of giving ownership of the class to nonprofessionals is a good one.

Some worry about the church getting out of control. Not me. I agree with Roland Allen, who writes:

> If we cannot control it, we ought . . . to rejoice that we cannot control it. For if we cannot control it, it is because it is too great, not because it is too small for us. The great things of God are beyond our control. Therein lies a vast hope. Spontaneous expansion could fill the continents with the knowledge of Christ: our control cannot reach as far as that. We constantly bewail our limitations: open doors unentered; doors closed to us as foreign missionaries; fields white to the harvest which we cannot reap. Spontaneous expansion could enter open doors, force closed ones, and reap those white fields. Our control cannot: it can only appeal pitifully for more men to maintain control.[1]

I, too, long for a movement of God that is out of human control. If you are a pastor or church leader, it is hard to release control. But we must if we want to see the rapid, spontaneous expansion of the church. But what if people are about to make a mistake? Shouldn't we stop them? Shouldn't we help them? Well, it depends.

One of the things I appreciate about my parents is that they let me make some mistakes. I know they saw some coming. I know they could have stopped me. They could have stopped me in the name of helping me. But they knew better. They knew I would learn better if I learned from my own mistakes. So, if it wasn't going to kill me, they let me bloody my nose a bit.

I think good pastors do the same thing. They let their people take ownership of the ministry. Pastors, don't hog all the mistakes. Let your people make some of them.

> *People will get far more excited about their "dumb" ideas than my "brilliant" ones.*

Some of the mistakes I've let people make turned out to be not so bad after all. I once had a group that was growing to the point that it needed to reproduce, to divide into two smaller groups. They talked about all kinds of ways to do it. Finally, they came up with the idea of a 7:30 a.m. Sunday school class, before the 8:30 worship service. I thought it was a really bad idea. I hate mornings. Who would want to get up at 7:30 to do anything? I wasn't even sure God was up at that time in the morning! But I let them go ahead with their dumb idea. Do you know what? Years later that 7:30 a.m. early bird class is still going strong! Through that experience I learned that people will get far more excited about their "dumb" ideas than my "brilliant" ones.

Classes can organize themselves any way they think will get the job done. They set their own goals and agenda. They run their own classes in their own way. They own them.

Teachers, with authority comes responsibility. God is going to hold you responsible for your management of your class. Ultimately you work for him, not for your pastor or your church. Who are you tempted to blame for restricting the growth of your class? As long as you can blame someone else, you can let yourself off the hook. Maturity, however, begins with taking responsibility for your own life.

Ownership is the key to motivation. No one washes rental cars. If we want to see this nation reached for God, we must turn the ministry over to nonprofessionals. We must help them in their ministries instead of asking them to help us with ours. If we give them ownership of the ministry, they will have the motivation to double their classes every two years or less. We can reach our cities for Christ with groups like that. We can do all things through Christ, who gives us strength.

> *Ownership is the key to motivation. No one washes rental cars.*

Take a moment to tell God you are taking responsibility for the ministry he gave you. In the next chapter, you'll see that you can do the job that God has set before you. But faith is a necessary starting point to getting the job done.

NOTES

[1]Roland Allen, *The Spontaneous Expansion of the Church* (Grand Rapids, MI: Eerdmans, 1962), 13.

You Can Do It!

> *The need of the hour is for people to believe that God is God and that he can accomplish every promise he has ever made.*

Chapter 1 dealt with the worthiness of our goal, pointing out that if every class in America would double in two years or less we would reach America in just a few years. God has commanded us to make disciples of all nations. This is indeed a worthy goal. Chapter 2 showed that a class of ten needs to add only one person per quarter to accomplish this goal. However, I challenged you to thoroughly assimilate two per quarter. This goal is, I believe, both worthy and attainable. Finally, in chapter 3 we looked at the important concept of giving people personal ownership of their ministries, of helping them in their ministries instead of asking them to help us in ours.

Before we begin to discuss the means of doubling your class in two years or less, I want to remind you of two things:

● You can do it! God delights in using ordinary people to do extraordinary things.

● You must believe you can do it. God delights in using people of faith.

The need of the hour is for people to believe that God is God and that he can accomplish every promise he has ever made. Paul stresses both of these truths in 2 Corinthians 4:1-2, 7:

> Therefore, since through God's mercy we have this ministry, we do not lose heart. Rather, we have renounced secret and shameful ways; we do not use deception, nor do we distort the word of God. On the contrary, by setting forth the truth plainly we commend ourselves to every man's conscience in the sight of God...But we have this treasure in jars of clay to show that this all-surpassing power is from God and not from us.

Years ago, Howard Hendricks paraphrased verse 7 as follows, "We hold this treasure in common peanut butter jars." I think that captures the spirit of what Paul was saying. Not ornate glassware. Not fancy vases. Common peanut butter jars.

Of course, this raises the question "Why put something as precious as the gospel in something as ordinary as peanut butter jars?" If the gospel is the most important message known to humankind, if it is our most valuable possession, why put it in ordinary peanut butter jars?

One answer is, "Peanut butter jars are all God had to work with." There is an old saying that God must love ordinary people because he created so many of them.

God must love ordinary people because he created so many of them.

But there is another answer, one that has deep theological significance. It is very important to God that people never confuse the jar with the contents of the jar. He never wants people to look at the frame instead of the picture. So he uses ordinary people such as you and me to assure himself of receiving the glory.

This is why he uses ordinary people instead of professionals to get the job done. The role of professionals is to help the people be effective in their ministries. God wants to take the world for him through unpaid ministers who are being trained by professionals.

It may be hard for you to believe that you could be a part of God's means of reaching a city and then a country for Christ. If it is hard to believe, congratulations! You're a good candidate for the job. You see, God does not want people who see themselves as sharp enough to do God some good. He wants people who are humble enough to realize that without him we can do nothing (John 15:5).

The "catch" is, we must believe. Jesus told the blind men, "According to your faith will it be done to you" (Matthew 9:29). In the same way, we will see it when we believe it, not the other way around. God needs people who are confident that he can use them, for without faith, it is impossible to please God (Hebrews 11:6).

We will see it when we believe it, not the other way around.

We understand the faith needed for salvation. We understand the kind of faith that believes that God can save and forgive us of our sins. We also need to believe that God can do through us what he told us to do: make disciples of all nations.

Consider James 5:17: "Elijah was a man just like us. He prayed earnestly that it would not rain, and it did not rain on the land for three and a half years." If you really believe that Elijah was a man just like us, I invite you to embrace this kind of faith. God blesses people of great faith.

This is what amazed the world about the early church, that God was using normal peanut butter jars to get the job done. Acts 4:13 states,

"When they saw the courage of Peter and John and realized that they were *unschooled, ordinary men,* they were astonished and they took note that these men had been with Jesus" (emphasis mine).

What do you dream of God doing? What do you dream of God doing through you? People with great dreams are people who are used mightily of God. People are attracted to great dreams. Dreams are the birthplace of all accomplishments. Sometimes people say, "He probably never dreamed this would come of what he did." I doubt that this is often the case. It is more likely that things happened precisely because someone dared to dream.

> *When God wants to invite guests to a great banquet, a gala affair replete with all the trimmings, he goes to the* generic food aisle *to pick up the ingredients.*

I am convinced that, when God wants to invite guests to a great banquet, a gala affair replete with all the trimmings, he goes to the *generic food aisle* to pick up the ingredients. That's just the way he works. And when God wants to start a mighty movement of drawing men and women and boys and girls to himself, he uses ordinary people with extraordinary dreams. He puts the gospel in common peanut butter jars.

Section Two:
The Means—

TIGER!

*T***each a halfway decent lesson each and every week—nothing less will do.**

*I***nvite every member and every prospect to every fellowship every month.**

*G***ive Friday nights to Jesus.**

*E***ncourage the group to ministry.**

*R***eproduce new groups.**

Teach a halfway decent lesson each and every week—nothing less will do.

Small-group work must begin with teaching. We do not have to be incredible teachers; God can use ordinary people. We do need to understand and apply the basics of good communication.

Growth Principle #1: Quality Is More Important Than Quantity

I use two guiding principles to evaluate my effectiveness as a leader in Sunday school and small-group work. Chapter 6 will discuss the second principle. In this chapter, we'll look at the first:

Quality is more important than quantity.

By "quality" I mean the quality of the lives we are producing. Jesus has called us to make disciples, not just converts. If I cannot point to women and men, girls and boys, young people and senior adults whose lives are being changed, then I have failed, no matter how pretty the growth graph might be. I want to see people who are seeking to live the Christian life; who are having regular times alone with God; whose prayer lives are solid; who have a growing grasp of the Scriptures; whose families are hothouses of love, romance, and encouragement; and who are learning to serve in the area of their spiritual gifts. "Do the people I'm leading enjoy God?" is a better question than "How many did you have in class on Sunday?" The most impressive graphs and astonishing statistics in the world are wood, hay, and stubble if I cannot name people who are living the disciple's life.

We should never be content with impressive graphs and unchanged lives. Discipleship is the point. Godliness is the point. People who enjoy God more than the things of this world—that's what we're after. You can draw a crowd almost overnight with some of the strategies I will show you. The point, however, is not impressive graphs—it is godly people.

> *People who enjoy God more than the things of this world— that's what we're after.*

My father tells the story of a man who, by his own admission, was a bad man, a wicked man. He described himself as one who used to womanize, get drunk, and fight. Then he placed his faith in Jesus Christ. In one of the most telling descriptions I have ever heard, his son (who was not a believer at the time) said of his father that he "had a new man inside of him." You see, the son had never read 2 Corinthians 5:17. He did not know that "if anyone is in Christ he is a new creation." But he saw a new man living in his father. That's what we are after. Do the people you teach show visible evidence of having a new person inside?

> *Our job in Christian education is not to make smarter sinners. Our job is to make disciples.*

We are in the change business. Some people do not like change, but we are in that business. We are making disciples out of pagans, worshipers out of rebels, saints out of sinners, Christians out of heathens. We are out to make the cruel, kind; the haughty, humble; the profane, pious. Our job in Christian education is not to make smarter sinners. Our job is to make disciples.

It has always been curious to me that churches never report this one thing. We measure budgets, building costs, Sunday school attendance, participants in the music program, members of ladies' organizations, and so on. But we are never asked to answer the question "How many disciples did you make this year?" Perhaps this is because true discipleship is difficult to define, much less measure. There are some things we can measure: attendance, giving, how often people set aside time to read their Bibles, and how many verses they memorize. But externals are not the entire picture. The Pharisees would have done well on this kind of system. What we should seek to produce is people who enjoy God. How do you measure that?

Defining discipleship is a little like defining good music. I do not know exactly what makes good music, but I know it when I hear it. I do not know exactly what makes a disciple, but I know one when I see one. Musicians can define some objective criteria concerning good music. They understand that good music obeys certain rules of music theory. It pays attention to rules about keys and rhythms and so on. But music is more than that. And music can obey all the rules and still be bad.

What is a disciple? What does she look like? What attitudes does he portray? What skills does she possess? How does he spend his time? What are her priorities? Without a clear answer to these questions, we are working in a fog. We are painting a picture without a clear image in our minds of what the picture should look like. We may win with the numbers, but we lose where it really counts. Unless I can point to women and men, boys and girls whose lives have been radically changed by the gospel, I have not done what my Lord told me to do.

In *Disciple*, Juan Carlos Ortiz observes that if we have two hundred baby Christians one year and six hundred baby Christians a year later, we are not really growing. He warns against promoting the permanent childhood of the believer.[1] To avoid this, we need to know what a disciple is and how to make one.

So what is a disciple? Jesus outlines the answer to this question in three passages from the book of John. The first is John 8:31: "If you hold to my teaching, you are really my disciples." It is interesting that Jesus says this to those who already believed in him. The Greek word for "hold" is used in other contexts to mean "to abide, to live, to dwell, to be at home."[2] Therefore, those who have a firm grasp of God's Word and make it their home are on their way to being Christ's disciples. This is the first mark of a disciple: abiding in Christ and his Word. The second mark has to do with the body.

In John 13:35, Jesus explains, "By this all men will know that you are my disciples, if you love one another." This is such a direct statement that it needs no explanation. If the members of your group are characterized by love for one another, you are doing your job of making disciples.

I have asked a number of classes if they thought outsiders perceived believers to be more loving or less loving than the world in general. The resounding answer I have received is that there is little difference, that we are no more loving than the world. In many cases, the world perceives us as being more judgmental, critical, and condemning. No wonder we are not reaching people with the gospel. The world would beat our doors down if they thought they could find love here. You

The world would beat our doors down if they thought they could find love here.

couldn't build buildings fast enough; you wouldn't be able to start services often enough—the nets would be bursting if you could create a church that truly loved. I am not talking about some ethereal, high-sounding, out-there love. I am talking about the love that has someone over for dinner. I am talking about the love that gives a cup of cold water... or iced tea.

The first characteristic of a disciple is abiding in Christ; the second is love for other Christians. The third mark of a disciple is found in John 15:8. There Jesus states, "This is to my Father's glory, that you bear much fruit, showing yourselves to be my disciples." Eugene Peterson paraphrases this verse in a beautiful way: "When you're joined with me and

I with you, the relation intimate and organic, the harvest is sure to be abundant. Separated, you can't produce a thing."[3]

Included within the idea of fruit-bearing is reproduction. The seed is always in the fruit, and one of the marks of a mature fruit is the ability to produce more of the same. Likewise, you as a disciple should be producing more disciples, who should be producing more disciples, and so on. (More on this in Chapters 26 and 27.)

If you have ten lukewarm class members today and twenty lukewarm class members in two years, have you really accomplished all that much?

How about you? Can you give me the names, addresses, and phone numbers of people who are living for God? Can you point to people who are living the disciple's life Jesus described? If not, don't feel guilty. The gospel is all about grace, and forgiveness is available. But work on quality before quantity. Make sure you have disciples before you reproduce what you have. The last thing we want is to double a class full of lukewarm or immature believers. Groups reproduce in like kind. If we don't have disciples, we cannot reproduce disciples. If you have ten lukewarm class members today and twenty lukewarm class members in two years, have you really accomplished all that much?

On the other hand, if you have ten mature believers today and a year later all you have is ten even more mature believers, you have not been obedient to what Christ told you to do. Quantity is also important. We will explore the issue of quantity later on. But before we do, let's look at the process of producing disciples through our teaching. In order to produce quality disciples, you must produce a halfway decent lesson each and every week; nothing less will do.

NOTES

[1] Juan Carlos Ortiz, *Disciple* (Carol Stream, IL: Creation House, 1975), 85.
[2] See Luke 8:27; John 1:38; 7:9; and Acts 28:16. See also Craig S. Keener, *The IVP Bible Background Commentary: New Testament* (Downers Grove, IL: InterVarsity, 1993), 301.
[3] Eugene H. Peterson, *The Message* (Colorado Springs, CO: NavPress, 1993), 221.

The Importance of a Halfway Decent Lesson

The number one variable in predicting the growth of a class is the teaching ability of the teacher. If someone is not doing a good job with the teaching, no amount of outreach will be enough to grow a class and disciples will not be made. We need quality teaching to make quality disciples.

> *The number one variable in predicting the growth of a class is the teaching ability of the teacher.*

On the other hand, groups that have quality teaching seem to grow almost automatically. Jesus attracted huge crowds. This was, in part, because he was such a masterful teacher. Good outreach can accelerate the growth even further, but we must have the basis of good teaching in order to grow a group. Notice that I'm saying "good teaching"—it does not have to be sensational.

I take great comfort in knowing that I do not have to hit home runs with every lesson. I do, however, need to hit singles regularly. If people are not hearing something meaningful and applicable to them, you will not keep them, no matter how often you invite them. The lessons do not have to be the greatest ever, but they must meet needs.

If you want a church to grow, somebody had better be saying something helpful every Sunday morning. Nothing can replace good content. Would you be attracted to a church that had great programs, nice music, a huge advertising budget, but lousy sermons? People may stay in a church like that if they have a strong network of friends. They will stay reluctantly, however.

The same is true of small groups. You may have all the invitations, parties, and games you need to gather a crowd. But if someone is not saying something helpful to the group, people will not come back. In the long run, good advertising will never cover for a bad product. The label is important, but it's what is in the bottle that counts. Even if people do stay, they will probably not become disciples. It is the truth that sets people free. We are transformed by the renewing of our minds. Consequently, the disciple-making process depends on halfway decent teaching.

Thom Rainer's research bears this out: "One significant study done by and for mainline denominations found that in-depth teaching and preaching of orthodox Christian belief was *the single best predictor of church participation.* Strong Sunday Schools and scripturally-authoritative preaching engendered long-term health for the church."[1] We must have halfway decent teaching.

In the numerous church-growth conferences I have attended, speakers never talk loudly enough about the importance of preaching and teaching. Humility forbids them. Bill Hybels cannot stand up at his church-growth conference and say, "If you would just speak as well as I do, growth would take care of itself." Yet when I hear Bill Hybels speak, I know that his skill as a communicator is a crucial factor in the growth of Willow Creek Community Church.

> *You do not have to be Chuck Swindoll to grow a class.*

Consequently, some will object that I am not casting a high enough vision. In fact, some people have told me that we should ask for better than halfway decent teaching, that we want excellent teaching. They would like me to say that only fantastic teaching will grow a class. There is no doubt that excellent teaching can help and is, in some sense, our goal. I would like you to teach as well as you possibly can. But I also want to lend confidence to you if you are not Bill Hybels or Chuck Swindoll. You do not have to be Chuck Swindoll to grow a class. I am trying, in this chapter, to maintain a delicate balance between emphasizing the importance of good teaching and lending confidence to the teacher of average skill.

I have seen teachers who are so good that they can grow a class without applying many of the principles taught in this book. But they are rare. May I be honest with you? You are probably not that good. I know I'm not. But you are probably good enough to grow a class. Good enough to double that class every two years or less. Good enough to be used greatly by God.

Consider your favorite fast-food restaurant. Do you go there because it sells the greatest hamburgers in the world? Would you give it a ten on a scale of one to ten? Would you give it even a soft eight? I don't think so. I have asked groups all over the nation to rate fast-food hamburgers on a scale of one to ten. They usually get about a four or a five. That is halfway decent. But halfway decent hamburgers are good enough to make them popular. The halfway decent hamburger is sold around the world in clean stores, with good service, and through good advertising. And halfway decent lessons can be "sold" with good social gatherings and outreach. But they have to be at least halfway decent.

They cannot be like the lesson I heard one teacher present. The lesson was on John 17:12, which refers to Judas as the "son of perdition." (The word "perdition" means "under condemnation.") This is how the teacher approached the text: "Predestination. Who really understands predestination?" We have to do better than that! First of all, the word is perdition, not predestination. Second, you need to come up with something better than "Who really understands..." I have observed a lot of Sunday school teachers over the years, and, unfortunately, some of them are teaching on this level. We must do better than this if we are going to double our groups every two years or less.

If you can do better than halfway decent, great. Strive for excellence. But you need to hit at least a single just about every time you come to the plate.[2] Central to the process of creating disciples is delivering solid, halfway decent lessons each and every week. Nothing less will do. Because halfway decent teaching is so important, I will discuss in the next chapter the ten essential qualities of good teaching.

NOTES

[1] Thom S. Rainer, *Giant Awakenings* (Nashville, TN: Broadman and Holman, 1995), 177. Emphasis added.

[2] It is beyond the scope of this work to do an exhaustive treatment of great teaching. For that, I recommend *The 7 Laws of the Learner* by Bruce H. Wilkinson (Multnomah Press, 1992). It is available in both book and video format, and it is quite a bit better than halfway decent. It is incredible.

Ten Marks of Great Teaching

According to Plato, an unexamined life is not worth living. Unexamined teaching isn't all that great either. If you want to improve your teaching, begin by evaluating it:

- What do you do well?
- What comes naturally for you?
- With what do you struggle?

Evaluation is the beginning point of any improvement process.

I use ten characteristics to evaluate whether or not a lesson is good. Every one of these does not have to be in every lesson. Build on your strengths. The quickest way to improve your teaching is not to focus on making your weaknesses better. Rather, the fastest way to improve your teaching is to make your strengths stronger. Work on overcoming your weaknesses as well, but concentrate on maximizing your strengths. Here are ten benchmarks of great teaching. Use them as plumb lines to evaluate your teaching.

1. Passion

> "It is a sin to bore people with the gospel."
> Howard Hendricks

Did you present the truth with some fire? If the truth does not matter to you, it will not matter to them. Howard Hendricks is fond of saying, "If you are going to bore people, don't bore them with the gospel. Bore them with calculus, bore them with earth science, bore them with world history. But it is a sin to bore people with the gospel." Someone once asked Charles Spurgeon, "What is the secret of great preaching?" He replied, "Get on fire with the gospel, and people will come to watch you burn." This was also the experience of the writer of Psalm 39:3: "My heart grew hot within me, and as I meditated, the fire burned; then I spoke with my tongue." This ought to be the goal of every teacher: to cultivate a hot heart before you speak.

I have seen teachers with mediocre content who spoke with such conviction that you just had to listen. But it is not a matter of either-or.

You can have good content and communicate it with passion. That is teaching at its best. Apollos was an example of accuracy and fervor. According to Acts 18:25, Apollos "had been instructed in the way of the Lord, and he spoke with *great fervor* and taught about Jesus *accurately*, though he knew only the baptism of John" (emphasis added).

It is possible, of course, to have a passionate heart and not show it. More often than not, gestures and voice inflection need to be overdone in order to come across at all. Animation in teaching is like stage makeup. The point is not to look like you have makeup on—it is to look normal. But if you are not wearing makeup when you are on stage, you will look flat. In a similar way, the point of animation in teaching is not so much to appear animated but to appear normal. If you use a normal voice in teaching, you will probably sound flat (read: boring). Very few teachers are too animated, so err on the side of overdoing it. Ultimately, the point is not how fired-up you appear, but how fired-up you really are. How excited are you about the grace of God?

I close with my favorite verse in Romans. Note that this is a command: "Never be lacking in zeal, but keep your spiritual fervor, serving the Lord" (Romans 12:11). Rate yourself on a scale of one to ten. How passionate are you in your teaching of the greatest news ever?

> *Passion*
> *Evaluation*
> *On a scale of*
> *one to ten,*
> *how passion-*
> *ate are you in*
> *your teaching?*

2. Practicality

Imagine yourself teaching your group this weekend. Now, in your imagination, write the following question in red paint on each person's forehead: "So what?" If your students weren't so polite, they would ask the question out loud. It's what they want to know: "What difference should this truth make to my Monday morning?" If you do not have a ready answer to that question, go back and study until you get one. Teaching is about application.

Did you provide specific ideas that can be applied to people's lives during the week? Did you teach for changed lives? People are not interested in accumulating information that does not relate to their lives. We are not out to make smarter sinners. We are seeking to change lives. Disciple-making is about application.

The key is to ask for small, specific, incremental changes. Do not push for monumental changes every week—just try to get a little bit of change

> *The key is to ask for small, specific, incremental changes.*

each week. Ask questions such as "What is one thing you could do this week to demonstrate your concern for the lost?" When someone says, "I could pray once for my neighbor John," make a hero out of that person. That is application that begins to make a difference, and it paves the way for further application. The ship begins to turn.

The application does not need to be "See ten people come to faith this week." That is good but too lofty for most people. It is like asking someone to high jump six feet. Most of us need to start with eighteen inches. Get people jumping over the bar before you move it higher. If the bar is perceived to be too high, people will not even attempt to jump it.

"Pray once this week" may be enough. Some application is better than no application at all. Application needs to be specific and have a time orientation. It needs to be something people can do this week. If it is something they are going to do next winter, when the kids are grown, or when they grow old, forget it. Application needs to be small, and it needs to happen this week.

It is also a good idea to ask each week about the application suggested the previous week. For example, you might say, "Last week we talked about praying for our non-Christian friends. Did anyone do this? What other steps could we take?" In an open group such as a Sunday school class or a cell group, accountability needs to be kept pretty simple. If you expect new people to feel comfortable in the group, don't hold people accountable for the last twenty-five verses they have been memorizing. Those kinds of intense, accountability-oriented discipleship groups are great for creating depth. But they are killers in providing an open place for people to come. Week-to-week accountability, however, will not run people off.

> *There is no place for condemnation in the Christian experience.*

Accountability needs to find the razor's edge of speaking the truth in love. If we communicate condemnation to those who fail (and everyone fails), we miss the gospel entirely. There is no place for condemnation in the Christian experience. There is, however, a place for truth spoken in love. So when someone says, "I want to have a quiet time five days this week, and I want you to hold me accountable," we need to do so.

I am familiar with one group leader who was holding a group accountable for daily quiet times. When the group failed in this, he would say, "That's OK—no big deal. I didn't have any quiet times this week either." That kind of accountability will not create disciples. We need to speak the truth in love. We need to communicate that disobedience never cancels grace, that it never calls into question God's love for us. But sin does have its consequences. We reap what we sow. The difference is that while condemnation says, "You are bad because you sinned," grace says, "You sinned. That is wrong. But there is grace. You are forgiven. You are accepted. You are loved."

In addition, there is a fine line between accountability and controlling. Accountability holds people accountable for their goals. Controlling attempts to manipulate people against their wills. The issue is not the goodness of the activity. The issue is: Who gets to decide? Suppose you tried to "hold people accountable" for not watching R-rated movies because you have a conviction about R-rated movies. Suppose you tried to hold them accountable even though they didn't share your convictions. That is not accountability. That is controlling. Accountability is holding people accountable for their goals. Paul said that "each one should be fully convinced in his own mind" about matters of personal conviction (Romans 14:5).

> *Accountability is holding people accountable for their goals.*

Bruce Wilkinson gives extensive treatment to the importance of application in *The 7 Laws of the Learner.* In the process, he tells of reading through and marking the manuscripts of great preachers in order to identify the portions that were application-oriented and the portions that were content-oriented. He discovered that the best preachers, now and in the past, averaged between 45 and 75 percent application.[1] Your teaching also should emphasize application.

Finally, application does not always have to involve doing. Sometimes the application might involve believing or feeling. The application of Psalm 23 is to believe that God is my shepherd and that I need not want. I am obedient to the truth of the psalm when I rest in God. On the other hand, the application of Philippians 4:4 ("Rejoice in the Lord always...") is to enjoy God. Many of the issues of Christian discipleship are issues of the heart. If we do not see this, we run the risk of being Pharisee-makers instead of disciple-makers. The Pharisees had application down to a science, but they missed the issues of the heart.

Evaluate yourself on how well you teach for application. Give yourself

Practicality Evaluation: Evaluate yourself on a scale of one to ten on how effectively you teach for application.

a ten if you teach for specific application every week. Give yourself a one if you hardly ever do so.

3. Humor

Were there instances when the group laughed together? Were there times when class members grabbed their sides, slapped their knees, threw back their heads, and laughed? Laughter is one of the best indicators of health in a group. When members of a group love one another, when they enjoy being together, when Christian fellowship is what it should be—people laugh. When there are tension and ill will in the body, however, no one laughs.

I am not talking about telling jokes. I am speaking of the spontaneous, unrehearsed laughter that bubbles up from healthy relationships. Nothing makes class more enjoyable than a little humor. Humor is the jam on the bagel.

You can often use humor to open up the group to receive God's truth. It helps people relax. Their guard comes down, and they become more

It ought to be fun to come to class.

responsive. You have probably had the experience, as I have, of laughing until your side hurt, only to find a sword in your side. A speaker had skillfully used the sword of the Spirit in such a way that you did not even know an incision had been made. Laughter was the anesthesia.

It ought to be fun to come to class. It should be more than fun—informative and life changing and all the rest—but it should be fun. Your class will tend to grow if people like to come to class.

Humor Evaluation Evaluate yourself on a scale of one to ten. How much humor do you allow in your class?

I am not talking about pretending to be a stand-up comedian. (If, however, you hear a good joke that relates to the topic, don't be afraid to use it.) The key is to allow humor when it comes; you don't have to plan it. Never force humor. Few things are as disgusting as someone trying to be funny who isn't. Forced humor is worse than no humor at all. But don't be so serious about studying the Word that you don't let people enjoy Christian fellowship and the pleasure of being together.

How well do you use humor in your class? Take a moment to rate yourself on a scale of one to ten.

4. A Personal Element

If you want to make your teaching interesting and effective, make it personal. Teaching that doesn't apply personally doesn't apply at all. Good teaching is not about vague, distant abstractions. God is personal, and the process of discipleship is personal. So ask yourself two questions:

- Did I touch them where *they* live?
- Was I open about *myself*?

You need to make the application personal to your group, and you need to be open enough to show how the truth works in your life. Do not use exclusively personal illustrations, but do use some. This is a small group. There is something inherently personal about small-group ministry. But you must set the tone for the rest of the group. They will generally be as transparent and open as you are. One reason we have small groups is so the universal message of the gospel can be personalized to the individual. Your job is to take the cloth and tailor it to fit the individual.

Being personal is also one of the best ways to create interest. People are interested in others—especially their personal lives. That is why the tabloids sell so well. A personal element is interesting. If you ever sense that people's interest is slipping, remember that one of the best ways to grab the group's attention is to tell how the truth applies personally to you.

> *People are interested in others—especially their personal lives.*

Of course, you don't want to take this too far. This is Sunday school, not therapy. Once I attended a group in which a member confessed to a previous life of prostitution. The group members were on the edge of their seats, holding their breath. Unfortunately, although her story held the interest of the group, she never came back. She felt too exposed and embarrassed to show herself again. She got caught up in the moment and became too transparent.

This is not what I am advocating. I am talking about being as open, as transparent, and as honest as you can be within the bounds of good sense and discretion. Unfortunately, my experience has been that most groups are not personal enough.

How well do you teach in a way that is personal and touches people

A Personal Element

Evaluate yourself on a scale of one to ten. Do you teach in a way that is personal and touches people where they live?

where they live? Honestly rate yourself on a scale of one to ten.

5. Involvement

Was everyone interested? Were they "with you"? Did most of the people participate in the discussion? Did over half of the group talk? Or were people looking at their watches?

One way to ensure people are involved is by asking questions to get the group talking. When *you* are talking, they may or may not be interested. When *they* are talking, you can be sure that they are interested. That is one of the advantages of asking questions. Later in this book, I will devote a whole chapter to the art of asking good questions.

Another way to get people involved is to have them work together to solve a problem or to complete a task. For example, you might give class members case studies or real-life situations to discuss and to resolve. People discussing how to counsel a friend being abused by her husband will be far more involved than those simply listening to a teacher lecture on general family problems and their biblical solutions. You might even have small groups read and discuss a biblical passage and then, in a creative way, teach the rest of the class what they learned. For example, groups might create objects that portray the goodness of God's creation (Genesis 1), write songs that tell others why God is worthy of praise (Psalm 113), or draw posters that represent the love we are to show to others (1 Corinthians 13). However you choose to do it, you can get people involved by getting them to work together.[2]

Involvement Evaluation

On a scale of one to ten, how involved and attentive was the group the last time you taught?

Of course, people can be involved without saying or doing anything. But when they are answering a question or sharing an experience, you can be almost sure they are paying attention. (Only very rarely can people talk and not listen to themselves, and these people are really difficult to teach.) But if people are not involved, they are not learning, you are not teaching, and disciples are not being formed.

Think about the last class you taught. If the group was involved and paying attention, give yourself a ten.

If it was obvious to you and everyone else that they were bored, give yourself a one.

6. Personal Preparation

Do you generally prepare well enough to present the lesson with confidence? Confidence is everything. You will never master every detail of even a short passage. That is the beauty of the Bible. We can never completely plumb the depths of its beauty and insight. But we do need to have a basic grasp of what is in the text. Don't be afraid to admit it when you don't know, but try to know as much as you can! Preparation shows itself both in content and in confidence.

You cannot look at a passage for the first time Saturday night and teach well Sunday morning.

One of the best ways to do this is to read the passage daily as part of your devotional discipline. Read it often so that you have a real feel for the text. Read it in several translations. Read it early in the week. Ask your friends questions about the text. Involve yourself in the text so you are very familiar with it and can speak confidently about what the text says.

Preparation that yields confidence cannot be done in the final hours. You cannot look at a passage for the first time Saturday night and teach well Sunday morning. Preparation that yields confidence is built slowly. Enjoy the passage. Learn from it. Let the Holy Spirit be your teacher before you are your group's teacher.

Evaluate your lesson preparation on a scale of one to ten. Is your preparation strong enough to give you a sense of confidence in teaching the passage?

Personal Preparation Evaluation: *On a scale of one to ten, is your preparation strong enough to give you a sense of confidence in teaching a passage?*

_____

7. Background

When you're teaching, do you reveal some interesting background not evident from a casual reading of the text? You need to know the text, but also you need to know what lies behind the text. You should be able to answer the questions the text asks. For example, suppose the subject of your teaching is Luke 13:4:

Or those eighteen who died when the tower in Siloam fell on them—do you think they were more guilty than all the others living in Jerusalem?

Here is an obvious question that you'd better know the answer to: What is the deal with this tower? As the teacher, you ought to give a simple, straightforward answer to this question without looking at any notes.

Sunday school needs to be more than a "pooling of ignorance." You will have a few people in your group who will have studied the lesson before class, and you should encourage them to do so. Still, you as the teacher need to bring that extra level of depth that makes the group feel it was worth coming because they learned something they did not know before.

The longer you work at this, the easier it becomes. One of the joys of studying the Bible is the accumulation of knowledge over years of study. But be careful! Our brains are buckets with holes in them (for some of us, they are mostly holes!). We need to make sure there is a constant input of fresh information. That is the joy of preparation. That is why many teachers love to spend money on books.

> ### Background Evaluation
> *Evaluate yourself on a scale of one to ten. Did you understand the background well enough to bring some fresh information to the discussion that is not obvious from a casual reading of the text?*

Think of your last lesson. Did you understand the background well enough to spice up the discussion with some fresh information that is not obvious from a casual reading of the text?

8. Introduction

Did you seize people's attention the moment you began? Did you begin the lesson with something that pulled them to the edges of their chairs and made them take notice? Or did some people secretly say to themselves, "Oh, gee-whiz, another Sunday school lesson. Yawn."

Two parts of the lesson ought to be especially well-prepared: the beginning and the end. Here are some tools you can use at the beginning to wake the group up and to get everyone's attention:

● a thought-provoking question such as "Is Christianity easy or hard?"[3]

● a heartwarming story such as the following: A boy was walking the seashore, picking up starfish and tossing them back into the ocean. When someone asked him what he was doing, he explained, "The starfish will dry out and die if they are not thrown back into the ocean." The beach was littered mile after mile with starfish. "You can't make a difference with all these starfish. Look around. They go on for miles." The boy was silent. Then he stooped down and lifted a drying starfish from the sand. With a flick of the wrist, he tossed it into the safety of the water, saving its life. "But I made a difference with that one," he replied.

- a small group discussion that draws on people's experiences such as situations in which they were asked to compromise their ethics, their favorite childhood memories, times they felt loved or unloved, or even their favorite movie characters.

Holding the group's attention for an entire hour is difficult enough. The easiest time to get their attention is at the beginning. If they do not lend you their attention then, they probably never will. Remember, if their minds are wandering, you are not making disciples.

On a scale of one to ten, do you normally come off the starting blocks with zest? Do you begin the lessons with attention-getting openings?

Introduction Evaluation: Rate yourself on a scale of one to ten. Do you normally come off the starting blocks with zest? Do you begin the lessons with attention-getting openings?

9. Inspiration

Teaching is more than telling people what happened or what ought to happen. It is inspiring people to do what they ought to do. You may not be the nation's best Christian motivator. You may not be Zig Ziglar, but you can learn from Zig Ziglar. People need, want, and crave inspiration. Motivation is 90 percent of almost everything, so don't be afraid to "preach a little." Challenge people to the worthy cause of living fully devoted lives for Christ.

Teaching is more than telling people what ought to happen.

Most of us *know* far more than we actually *do*. In most cases, the problem is not knowledge—it is motivation. To help people apply the truth to their lives, you must give them both the "how to" and the "want to."

There are two ways to motivate people: with a carrot and with a stick. For example, you can motivate by teaching the benefits of obedience (carrot) and the bad things that happen when we are not obedient (stick). It's not very motivating simply to be told that we ought to do something because it is right. Even the Bible teaches that faith has its rewards: "And without faith it is impossible to please God, because anyone who comes to him must believe that he exists and that he *rewards* those who earnestly seek him" (Hebrews 11:6, emphasis added). Teachers need to show what these rewards are. Giving has its rewards. Fidelity has its rewards. Honesty has its rewards. Write these rewards in large, colorful letters.

On the other hand, the Bible doesn't hesitate to warn of punishment, and neither should teachers. Warn class members that bad things will happen if they are unfaithful. Paint compelling word pictures about the pain of disobedience.

> *Inspiration Evaluation*
> *On a scale of one to ten, do you inspire the members of your group to do what they ought to do? Do you use an appropriate balance of carrot and stick?*

Inspiration also has a great deal to do with enthusiasm. People are not going to get any more excited about living the Christian life than you are about teaching your lesson. Motivate with enthusiasm. Remember, the Greek word from which "enthusiasm" derives means "God in me."

A final component of inspiration relates to your confidence in your class members. If you believe they can do it, they probably can. There is something highly motivating about having someone in your corner believing you can do something. Teach from a positive faith that we can do all things through Christ.

How well do you inspire people? Do you go beyond telling them what they ought to do? Do you inspire them to do what they ought to do? Do you use an appropriate balance of carrot and stick?

> *The great danger for many teachers is not that they say too little but that they say too much.*

10. Focus

When you teach, do you have one "big idea" that you attempt to drive home throughout the lesson? Do you hunt with a rifle or with a shotgun? The great danger for many teachers is not that they say too little but that they say too much. Your lesson needs to have a central focus, a big idea. If someone asked you before you walked into class, "What are you teaching today?" you ought to be able to respond in one sentence: "Today I will be teaching my class . . . " If you think this is an unrealistic goal, I challenge you to ask your pastor sometime, "What is the big idea of today's sermon?" Effective preachers will not stutter in their reply. One pastor I know asks his kids at Sunday lunch, "OK, kids, what was the big idea in today's sermon?" If they can give it to him, he feels he has done pretty well.

It's OK to chase a few rabbits from time to time, but drive to a central, focused verdict. When you teach, how often do you focus on a central idea? How often do you wander from point to point?

> **Focus Evaluation**
> *Evaluate yourself on a scale of one to ten. Do you concentrate on one central idea?*

The unexamined life is not worth living, and the unexamined teacher isn't so good either. Use these criteria to evaluate yourself regularly. On the following page is an evaluation sheet. Make copies, and evaluate yourself each week. If you are really brave, have your spouse or a class member do the evaluation with you. The fastest way to grow a class is to increase the effectiveness of the teaching. Every teacher can improve. You can. I can. Even Chuck Swindoll can. If you are going to double your class every two years or less, you have to teach a halfway decent lesson each and every week—nothing less will do.

NOTES

[1] Bruce H. Wilkinson, *The 7 Laws of the Learner* (Sisters, OR: Multnomah Press, 1992), 128.

[2] To learn more about using active learning to get people involved, see Thom and Joani Schultz, *Why Nobody Learns Much of Anything at Church: And How to Fix It* (Loveland, CO: Group Publishing, 1993).

[3] If people say that it's easy, ask them if it's always easy for them. If they say it's hard, ask them why Jesus says his yoke is easy (Matthew 11:30). The answer to this question is not as obvious as may seem.

Self-Evaluation

Rate yourself on a scale of one to ten,
with one being poor and ten being excellent.

_____ **Passion:** Did you present the truth with some conviction?

_____ **Practicality:** Did you provide specific ideas that can be applied to people's lives this week? Did you teach for a verdict?

_____ **Humor:** Were there times when the group laughed together?

_____ **A personal element:** Did you touch people where they live? Were you open about your own life?

_____ **Involvement:** Was everyone interested? Did a majority of the class participate in the discussion? Did you involve people in some sort of learning experience?

_____ **Personal preparation:** Did you prepare well enough to present the lesson with confidence?

_____ **Background:** Did you bring some interesting background information not evident from a casual reading of the text?

_____ **Introduction:** Did you grab people's attention at the very beginning?

_____ **Inspiration:** Did you attempt to inspire people to do what you wanted them to do?

_____ **Focus:** Did you have one "big idea" that you attempted to drive home throughout the lesson?

Honesty

Halfway decent teaching does more than present truth. It does more than invite application. Halfway decent teaching also heals. James 5:16 commands us, "Confess your sins to each other and pray for each other so that you may be healed."

Question: What is promised to people who confess their sins to God but to no one else? They are promised forgiveness, to be sure, but what about healing? None.

No healing is promised to people who confess their sins to God only. They are promised forgiveness (1 John 1:9), but nowhere are they promised healing. Forgiveness has to do with the past. Healing has to do with the future. Healing comes from confessing our brokenness within the context of a group or, at least, to another individual. To double our classes every two years, we must create environments in which healing can take place.

I define sin pretty broadly. When Isaiah saw his and the people's sin in the light of God's holiness, he cried, "Woe to me! I am ruined!" (Isaiah 6:5). The Hebrew word that is translated "ruined" means "undone" or "scattered." Isaiah was saying that his life was falling apart. That is what sin does: It sends our lives out of control. We do not have it together, as we would like to believe. Experiencing God will make us whole, but first we have to encounter God's holiness, which will make us miserable.

The problem is not just "sins"—a lie here or a lustful thought there. It is "sin"—that part of my life that is still operating in rebellion against God. It is the part of my life that isn't working, the part of my life that is broken. It is only when this brokenness is confessed to a friend and taken to God in prayer that we can find healing. If you want people in your Sunday school class to be well, help them be obedient to James 5:16.

> *We do not need to confess our brokenness to the entire world. But we do need a place where we can confess it to someone.*

This may or may not happen in class. If you have a large class, it is probably best that it not take place in class. We do not need to confess our brokenness to the entire world. But we do need a place where we can confess it to someone. All too often, however, we are guilty of "happy talk." "How are you?" "Fine, praise God! Everything is wonderful—hallelujah!" That is fine as long as it is honest. But if we are not well, we need a place to tell someone we are broken.

In the video series *Faith Has Its Reasons*, Rebecca Pippert tells the poignant story of experiencing this in a Harvard University psychology class. The professor wanted class members to get in touch with their feelings, so he divided the class into groups and asked them to share whatever was not working in their lives. They were amazingly honest. One shared of her depression, another of his frustration with his father, another of girlfriend troubles. Honesty. Reality.

Then Rebecca went across town to a Christian Bible study. It was filled with happy talk. Everything was wonderful with everyone. There were no problems because this was not a place where problems were allowed. The contrast was amazing. One group had all the problems but no answers. The other had all the answers but no problems. Unfortunately, God will not help us with problems we will not admit.

This type of honesty accounts for some of the healing that takes place in the psychological community. If you have the privilege of talking to someone who has been through therapy, you will hear stories of people being honest with each other in a group. People talk to counselors about what is really going on. They are honest. And their souls became whole.

> *Your job as group leader is to create an atmosphere in which people can be honest.*

Your job as group leader is to create an atmosphere in which people can be honest. It may or may not be in class; it may be over coffee during the week. But if people do not have a place in which they can be honest, they will not find help for their brokenness. No healing is offered to those who don't confess their sins to others.

Barriers to Honesty

What prevents us from being honest with each other? The benefits of honesty are obvious. We all crave intimacy. So why aren't we more honest with each other in class? Let me mention four causes.

First, the atmosphere is wrong. Our group may not feel like a place where we can really share. It's a place where we can talk about various theories of the creation, where we are going for Christmas holidays, or how our favorite football team is doing. But it may not feel like a place where we can talk about a marriage that is not working, kids who are breaking our hearts, or a Christianity that is not making a difference in our day-to-day lives. Maybe it is the cold walls or the hard folding-chairs or something else, but the atmosphere just feels wrong.

The answer is, of course, to create an atmosphere in which people feel free to share. Challenge your class to be honest. Allow your class to divide into small enough groups that people can be honest with one another. It may mean challenging class members to find two or three friends with whom they can meet regularly in their homes. It may mean encouraging clusters of three or four to gather over coffee each week.

A second barrier to honesty is lack of a pacesetter. In many cases, when one person is honest, the group follows. We often think we are the only ones with problems. But when we are bold enough to say, "This isn't working," we often discover others for whom it isn't working either. Like most things in life, being honest requires leadership. Speed of the leaders, speed of the team.

Trying to fix other people's problems is a third barrier to honesty. One of the interesting insights coming out of twelve-step literature is that it is counterproductive to try to fix each other. We can fix only ourselves. An atmosphere in which we are constantly trying to fix each other will quickly squelch honesty. I do not want a group that is constantly trying to fix me. It does not matter how well-meaning the group is in this. Fixing kills honesty.

I have seen this happen in groups time and time again. One person will bravely share something that is not working. Someone else will say, "You just need to pray more." Another will tell the person, "Just forgive and forget." Another will suggest, "Have more faith." Everyone has simple answers to enormous and complex problems...and no one puts a bandage on the wound. This is what gives Sunday school a bad name, when giving a "Sunday school answer" becomes synonymous with giving simplistic, unrealistic, or poorly thought-out answers.

People do this fixing in a well-meaning way. They are honestly trying to help...but it does not help. It only squelches honesty. There is something almost magical that Christians can do for one another. If they will hear one another, really listen to the feelings as well as the facts, and bring both together to the Father, the group will find healing. But as long as we are trying to fix each other, God isn't allowed to do much fixing.

James 5:16 does not say, "Confess your sins, do your best to fix each

> *Emotions are inherently amoral and should always be validated.*

other, and then pray." It is counterintuitive to what we think, but trying to fix things just messes them up. What we need to say is, "That must really hurt. I am sorry." Emotions are inherently amoral and should always be validated. Actions are moral; emotions are not. If I tell you I feel a certain way and you rebuff me by saying I shouldn't feel that way, I am not likely to share again. My emotions are not wrong. They are just feelings. Ethics has to do with behavior, not emotions. We need a place where we can hear each other say, "I understand why you would feel that way."

It is true that it is wrong to cultivate certain emotions. For example, it is wrong to cultivate lust and greed, which essentially are feelings. But it is not wrong for people to admit that they are fighting these feelings. In fact, we will never win the fight until we admit that there is a war.

> *Instead of trying to fix a person, try fixing a meal for a person.*

What we can do, instead of trying to fix, is to serve. Instead of trying to fix a person, try fixing a meal for a person. Pray for people. Send cards. Let your love be visible and tangible. But don't correct or scold. There is, of course, a place for admonition, but it is not in the context of the honest confession of sins.

A fourth reason we tend to be less than honest is because we have all been burned by a lack of confidentiality. A group that wants to be honest must let the things said in the group stay in the group. Nothing will kill honesty as quickly as gossip. If I hear you talking about someone else in an unflattering way, I will assume you'll do the same when you turn your back on me. If, on the other hand, you always speak well of others, putting them in the best possible light, I will be more likely to entrust myself to you.

If you ever violate my trust, I will never again share with you. We may continue to be friends, but I will not be open and honest with you. I can't.

I have come to a place in life where I long for a community in which we can be honest with each other. I think a lot of people long for that, too. No more superficiality. Only speaking the truth in love (Ephesians 4:15). That is what the church should be. Groups like that will have no trouble doubling in size every two years or less. Creating an atmosphere of honesty is essential to teaching a halfway decent lesson. It is essential to the process of making disciples. It is an essential part of an atmosphere in which people can find wholeness.

Smart People Listen

Robert Schuller wrote our best formula for success: "Find a need and fill it."[1] If you want to be successful as a teacher, concentrate on meeting needs. The question is, how do you discover what people need?

Ask them and then listen, listen, listen. Smart people listen. If you keep asking and, especially, keep listening, people will tell you the needs of their hearts. And if you concentrate on meeting those needs, you will never be without an audience. If needs are being met, people will beat a path to your door.

Different people want different things from a class. Some want historical background; others want a theological perspective. Many want practical help to everyday problems. Still others want psychological healing and comfort.

The problems that need to be addressed vary widely. Some people have honest intellectual problems. They see apparent contradictions between the Bible and life and want answers. Some are experiencing conflicts at home. They want a different kind of answer. People will have different questions according to their level of knowledge and situation. But if you listen, people will tell you everything you need to know to be the best teacher they ever had.

Because people learn in different ways, they do not all want the same kind of teachers. I have heard teachers that I did not care for at all but who were very popular with their students. These teachers knew something I didn't. They knew that the group wanted something I probably would not give them if I were there teacher. How did they learn this? They listened.

I mentioned earlier that for years I hammered away at the idea that we Christians do not have enough contact with people outside of the church. I had heard that the average Christian doesn't have any non-Christian contacts two years after coming to faith. So I preached on the importance of having non-Christian friends.

Then one morning I asked my class, "How many non-Christian friends do you have?" Their answer: five. On average, each had five non-Christian friends. In fact, I think the only one who didn't have five non-Christian friends was me! I had to listen to find this out.

Your class members may have 85 percent of their theology right.

They may understand the doctrines of biblical authority, the Trinity, and the last days. But they may need some help on the concept of grace. If you spend all their time on the things they know, they will become bored. How do you discover where your students' grasp of truth is soft? Smart people listen.

Much of scriptural truth is balancing truth. In order to build disciples, we need to know where our class tends to emphasize one side of the equation too heavily. How do we discover this? Smart people listen.

I listen to the people I love.

Listening does another thing. It communicates love. I listen to the people I love. In addition, by listening, we earn the right to be heard. Perhaps the lesson deals with James 1:19: "Everyone should be quick to listen, slow to speak, and slow to become angry." How long does it take to communicate that? Not very long.

But how long does it take to earn the right to say it in a way that communicates? People have an inborn sense of justice. If you listen to them, they will listen to you. If you spend thirty minutes listening to the people in your class, you can say toward the end of the hour, "Let me summarize what I think is really important in this passage." And they will hear you. That is why...smart people listen.

If you want to do a halfway decent job of teaching your class, listen to them. Find out what they know and what they don't know. Discover what they want and what they don't want. Listen to them, and you will be well on your way to becoming an excellent teacher.

NOTES

[1] Robert H. Schuller, *Your Church Has a Fantastic Future!* (Ventura, CA: Regal Books, 1986).

Good Question!
Why Asking Questions
Is the Best Way to Teach

May I confess my sin to you? I am far more interested in what I have to say than in what you have to say. I believe this is true of most people. We are all interested in ourselves and what we have to say, but we wonder if anyone else is interested in us and our ideas. We wonder if anyone cares. This is one reason asking questions is one of the best ways to teach.

> *I am far more interested in what I have to say than in what you have to say. I believe this is true of most people.*

It is difficult not to pay attention when you are talking. It is easy to doze off when someone else is speaking—even if that person is pretty interesting. This is another reason asking questions is the best way to teach adults. If you would become a halfway decent teacher, make lavish use of questions as a teaching method.

I believe in questions so much that I write out twenty-five to thirty questions for my teachers each week.[1] One of my goals is to write questions on the entire Bible. I believe in questions because they accomplish at least three things.

1. Questions involve the group.

When there is no involvement, there is no disciple-making. When there is no involvement, there is no change. When there is no involvement, there is no education.

> *When there is no involvement, there is no disciple-making.*

Let me be clear—it's possible to involve people without using questions. You can involve your group with lecture, storytelling, and various other methods. They might pay attention. But they are nearly guaranteed to listen to themselves. It is hard to daydream when you are talking. So why take a chance? If people are silently listening, they may or may not be involved. But when people are talking, it is unlikely they are secretly dozing off. *This is why it is a worthy goal to encourage each person in your group to*

> *It is a worthy goal to allow each person in your group to say something of significance to the rest of the class every week.*

say something of significance to the rest of the class every week.

2. Questions build relationships.

Small groups have several purposes, one of which is to make people smarter. There is no virtue in ignorance. People who attend over several years should learn something about God and the Bible. My personal goal is that anyone who sits under my teaching for two years or more would be able to tell the story of the Bible in a five-minute overview. I try to teach content. Small groups should also help people apply what they learn to their day-to-day lives. Group members should be challenged to live more ethically. They should be encouraged to pursue faith, love, and godly living. This is a second important purpose of groups.

A third, and equally important, purpose of small groups is to provide a place where people can build relationships. This is what I mean when I talk about the formation of little platoons. We should form relationships in class that continue throughout the week.

> *If the only purposes of groups were to make people smarter and more ethical, we could get videotapes that would do a far better job of lecturing than you or I could do.*

If the only purposes of groups were to make people smarter and more ethical, we could get videotapes that would do a far better job of lecturing than you or I could do. We cannot compete with the people who are available on videotape today. But videotapes do not form relationships. In addition, the discussion prompted by good questions not only helps you know the group better, it also lets the group know the group better. The truth is that most adults do not attend Sunday school because they have a burning desire to know more.[2] They would like to learn, but they also want to meet some friends. We live on a lonely planet.

And what better place to meet friends than in a small group? Where would you have people go to meet friends, if not to church? Groups that double every two years or less tend to be relationally tight. One of the best ways to build relationships is to ask lots of questions.

3. Questions help you discover what your class still needs to learn.

We don't normally give tests in our groups, but we still need to know what the people know and don't know. If you are presenting halfway decent lessons, your people already know quite a bit. But you won't know what they know without asking questions. Asking questions helps you discover the level of knowledge and maturity of the group.

I follow two principles that relate to this: I never attend a conference I could have taught, and I never read a book I could have written. In the same way, don't make your people attend a class they could have taught. You won't double your class every two years by going over the same old pool of knowledge. However, by asking lots of questions and carefully listening to people's answers, you will soon learn what areas need further emphasis. One of the best ways to become a halfway decent teacher is to ask lots of questions.

NOTES

[1] These are now available on my home page on the World Wide Web. My address is http://www.joshhunt.com.

[2] Dick Murray, *Strengthening the Adult Sunday School Class* (Nashville, TN: Abingdon, 1981), 26.

Creating Tension in Class

Have you ever noticed that it is nearly impossible to leave a good movie during the final five or ten minutes, but people gladly leave Sunday school five minutes before it's over to go sing in the choir? It never seems to bother them. They almost seem happy to slip out early.

Why is this, and what does it have to do with great teaching? For that matter, what do great movies, great books, and great teaching have in common?

They all have a cloud of whodunit hanging over them. You can't leave during the last five minutes of a movie because by that time you are so involved, so worked up, so curious that you just can't leave.

Amazing special effects, solid cinematography, and even great acting will rarely overcome a bad plot in a movie. A good plot keeps you guessing to the final moment how the whole thing will work out. The writers build in a problem that demands to be solved. We have to know whodunit.

Have you ever read a novel that you just couldn't put down? What are the chances of getting to the final four or five pages and just wandering off? It never happens. If the author has done his or her job, there is an atmosphere of suspense that will not let you go. It is that creative tension that keeps you turning pages until the very end.

> *Good teachers "create" more problems than they can solve.*

The same is true of good lessons. Good teachers "create" more problems than they can solve. That is what the light of the Word does—it creates problems. We didn't know what the problems were when they were in the dark. Our lives were like a messy garage with the light off. Now, with the light on, we can see the problems plainly. Good teaching does not simply provide solutions; it also creates problems. Until the problems are in the light, there can be no solutions.

Good teachers leave a little creative tension in the air the entire hour. They create an atmosphere that you can almost touch, an atmosphere that reaches out and makes you ask, "How will the teacher explain this one? What's the answer to this dilemma? How do I solve this mystery?

What is the solution?"

Mediocre teachers prefer to avoid tension at all costs. They like everything settled, everything neat, everything as it should be. They don't like any questions or any uncertainty. All is at peace. All is quiet. All are bored.

Skilled is the teacher who can employ creative tension. People dare not leave because they want to see how this whole thing turns out. People pay attention because they are curious. And if they look at their watches at all, it's only because they wonder how in the world the teacher will bring this thing to closure in the remaining time.

This is what makes a ballgame exciting: wondering who will win. No matter how exciting the play-by-play, if you already know the outcome, the predictability makes it boring. Too many Sunday school lessons are too predictable. We need an element of creative tension, a bit of who-dunit in every lesson.

Here is an example of creative tension in practice. Suppose the text for the day is Philippians 1:6: "Being confident of this, that he who began a good work in you will carry it on to completion until the day of Christ Jesus." A teacher could approach this text by simply reading the verse and explaining the meaning of all the words: the Greek for "confident," the history behind "good work," some cross-reference material on "completion," and so on. Or the teacher could create some tension at the beginning of class by asking, "Whose job is it to make sure we grow to maturity in the faith: ours? God's? the church's? the pastor's?"

Nine times out of ten, people will say that it is our job. If they do, read the verse to them and ask, "Then why does God say he will be responsible for our sanctification?" Get really quiet, and let them begin to chew. If, on the other hand, they beat you to the punch and quote Philippians 1:6, follow up by asking, "Then what is our role in sanctification?" or "Then is our role strictly passive, to 'let go and let God,' as some say? Suppose that our role in sanctification is strictly passive. Why, then, does Philippians 2:12 say to work out our salvation with fear and trembling? Does that sound passive? What about these verses?"[1]

> *Too many Sunday school lessons are too predictable. We need an element of creative tension, a bit of whodunit in every lesson.*

● Luke 13:24—"Make every effort to enter through the narrow door, because many, I tell you, will try to enter and will not be able to."

● Romans 14:19—"Let us therefore make every effort to do what leads to peace and to mutual edification."

● Hebrews 12:14—"Make every effort to live in peace with all men and to be holy; without holiness no one will see the Lord."

● 2 Peter 3:14—"So then, dear friends, since you are looking forward to this, make every effort to be found spotless, blameless, and at peace with him."

"The Bible cannot contradict itself. So why does Philippians teach that God is bringing our salvation to completion while these verses say we are to make every effort to move toward maturity?"

Long pause. Allow people to struggle. Don't solve the problem; create the problem, and then leave it with them. Make the problem as tough as you can: "Look at Hebrews 4:11. What are we to make every effort to do in this verse? How do you make an effort to rest?"

Pause between each of these questions, and let the group think. Let people discuss the questions. If there are more than six in the group, form smaller groups of two, three, or four. Encourage real dialogue. Allow people to fight just a bit. Don't let it get ugly, but make sure that the discussion is real. Let some real creative tension develop. Force people to grapple with problems before you offer any answers.

When they start to settle on a conclusion, rattle them with another verse, perhaps Hebrews 13:17: "Obey your leaders and submit to their authority. They keep watch over you as men who must give an account. Obey them so that their work will be a joy, not a burden, for that would be of no advantage to you." Ask, "What are leaders responsible for? Doesn't this passage teach that it is neither God's responsibility nor our responsibility but the responsibility of those in leadership to bring us to maturity? How do you explain this?"

Keep quiet, and let them chew on it. No one will look at his or her watch. No one will yawn. No one will leave early for choir. You might make an enemy of your choir leader, but so be it.

I contrast this method with a lesson my dad once heard. The text was the story of the rich young ruler (Matthew 19:16-24). The story begs to stimulate controversy, to create tension. But not this day, not in this class. After reading the text, the teacher explained, "Now, this passage, of course, doesn't really mean we should give everything away. No—we should all tithe, of course, and give a little extra from time to time, but God doesn't expect all his children to give up everything they own to follow him. Why, that would be works theology, and we all know that isn't right."

Everyone nodded in agreement. Everyone felt better. Another discomforting passage of Scripture had been successfully laid to rest. All was at peace.

If I had been teaching that class, I would have asked: "Why does Luke 14:33 say, 'Any of you who does not give up everything he has cannot be my disciple'?" Then I'd keep quiet and let them think about it. If they came to an answer too quickly, I would press them harder. Make them squirm. Make them think. That is how disciples are made.

> *Make them squirm. Make them think. That is how disciples are made.*

By the way, please observe that this teacher's theology was orthodox. It is generally believed that God does not expect every believer to give away everything he or she owns. I have no quarrels with the teacher's theology. But there are far better ways to teach this story. I think the rich young ruler squirmed in front of Jesus, and we ought to squirm when we talk about him.

Toward the end of class, you can relieve the tension you have created with a simple summary. You might say, for example, "God may not ask every Christian to give everything away, but he wants every believer to be willing to give up everything. Sometimes God will come into our lives, place his hand on something of value, and ask, 'Do you love me more than this?' We need to be willing to say yes. Let me ask you to bow your heads. For the next ninety seconds, ask God this question: 'Is there anything that I have withheld from you that you would ask of me? anything of my time? my talents? my possessions? I lay it all on the altar again. As Abraham placed Isaac on the altar, I place everything I have on the altar. Do with my life what you will. I give complete control to you.' "

Unresolved tension

At times you might want to leave the group with the tension unresolved. Leave people wondering. Leave them asking. Leave them talking. If you study the teaching style of Jesus, you'll discover that he left a lot of things unanswered. Most teachers, on the other hand, want everything to be tidy and neat.

Has anyone ever called you during the week and said, "Teacher, I've been thinking all week about our lesson, and I think I have some insight into it. Have you ever considered..." When someone does this, you know that learning is taking place.

You might think that this approach will get old if you use it week after week. You may fear that, after a while, people will get used to this tension-resolution pattern, that they will not involve themselves in the tension because they know that a resolution is certain. One would think that they might, but they don't.

I have a friend who is a Western novel buff. After he curls up for a weekend with a good Western novel, his wife will often ask, "Well, did the hero get the villain and ride off with girl?" Smiling, he echoes, "Yeah, the hero got the villain and rode off with the girl." "Good." She squeezes his hand and smiles. All is as it should be. The hero and the girl rode off into the sunset together. Next weekend, my friend will read another Western novel. He simply has to find out whodunit.

In the same way, creative tension in class never gets old. It is effective week after week. If you want to double your group every two years or less, employ creative tension in your teaching. It will help you become more than a halfway decent teacher.

NOTES

[1] You may want to write the verses on slips of paper before class and pass them out for people to read or have people look up the verses in their own Bibles. You could also use Ephesians 4:3; Hebrews 4:11; and 2 Peter 1:5, 15.

Invite every member and every prospect to every fellowship every month.

In addition to halfway decent teaching each and every week, you need a strategy for reaching people. Inviting every member and every prospect to every fellowship every month is a proven strategy that flat works.

Growth Principle #2: Principle #1 Is Just Barely True

Two foundational principles guide my thinking about Sunday school and small group work. Principle #1: Quality is more important than quantity. Principle #2: Principle #1 is just barely true! That is to say, quantity—measurable, numerical, graphable growth—is also important. Consider the following verses from Acts:

- "Those who accepted his message were baptized, and about three thousand were added to their number that day" (2:41).
- "The Lord added to their number daily those who were being saved" (2:47).
- "But many who heard the message believed, and the number of men grew to about five thousand" (4:4).
- "More and more men and women believed in the Lord and were added to their number" (5:14).
- "The number of disciples in Jerusalem increased rapidly" (6:7).
- "Then the church throughout Judea, Galilee and Samaria ... grew in numbers, living in the fear of the Lord" (9:31).
- "The Lord's hand was with them, and a great number of people believed and turned to the Lord" (11:21).
- "A great number of people were brought to the Lord" (11:24).

> **Principle #1:** Quality is more important than quantity. **Principle #2:** Principle #1 is just barely true!

It's hard to understand some people's hesitancy toward numbers. Granted, numbers can be and have been abused. Perhaps people fear they will turn into a number. However, this is really not a realistic fear. People do not turn into numbers. No one has ever turned into a number. People have treated others as if they do not count, but no one has ever turned into a number.

Still, there have been abuses. At times numbers have been used to feed the egos of megalomaniacs. In addition, numbers have been misused to treat people impersonally. But most

60

of us don't stop using pianos simply because some people use pianos in bars. And if you are opposed to numbers, how do you say the first five books of the Bible: "Genesis, Exodus, Leviticus, N-n-n-n, Deuteronomy"? There is nothing inherently wrong with numbers or with growth.

There are numerous theories about church growth, with as many exceptions as there are principles. In fact, one of the cardinal principles of church growth is that every principle has an exception. Every principle except this one: In order to grow, you must want to grow. Very seldom will sustained growth occur without desire. We may not agree on exactly how to grow a class, but we can agree on this: A class ought to grow. This is the necessary starting point.

This desire must become very personal. You must be highly committed to wanting your group to grow. You should have a deep conviction that says, "My class ought to grow! The corporate life of this group should and must result in measurable, graphable growth." Until you have this "want to," not much will happen. You can double your class in two years or less, but you must *want* to do so.

Warren Bennis and Burt Nanus uncovered some fascinating insights from a study of ninety top leaders in America. Researchers spent extensive time with each person to discover the common secret of their success. But as they began to sift the data, they became frustrated.

> There seemed to be no obvious patterns for their success. They were right-brained and left-brained, tall and short, fat and thin, articulate and inarticulate, assertive and retiring, dressed for success and dressed for failure, participative and autocratic. There were more variations than themes.[1]

Then, a commonality began to surface:

> All ninety people interviewed had an *agenda*, an unparalleled concern with outcome. Leaders are the most results-oriented individuals in the world, and results get attention. Their visions or intentions are compelling and pull people toward them...These intense personalities do not have to coerce people to pay attention...they draw others in.[2]

In the coming chapters, we will look at specific methods and principles for doubling your class in two years or less. But first, I want to ask you to come along with me in making obedience to the Great Commission the ambition of your life. What better cause could you devote yourself to?

Take a moment to answer the following questions: Do I really want to obey Jesus' command to make disciples of all peoples? Do I want my class to double in two years or less? Set this book down, and don't pick it up until you have an answer. I hope your answer is yes. You can double your class in two years or less if you really want to. I can teach you how to do it, but you must begin with the desire to obey Jesus' command to make disciples of all people.

NOTES

[1] Warren Bennis and Burt Nanus, *Leaders* (New York, NY: Harper & Row, 1985), 25-26.
[2] Bennis and Nanus, *Leaders*, 28.

Ice Cream and Evangelism

Donald McGavran, the founder of the modern church-growth movement, laid the groundwork for all church-growth thinking that was to follow. One of his key insights was that most of the barriers to the gospel are not theological; they are social.[1] Or, to paraphrase Juan Carlos Ortiz, most people who are opposed to the gospel are not opposed to ice cream.[2]

> *Most people who are opposed to the gospel are not opposed to ice cream.*

The greatest unmet need in your community is love. People crave fellowship and love.[3] They want to know and to be known, to love and to be loved. They want to socialize—to talk and listen and share and laugh. They want close, personal friends with whom they can be totally honest. They also want a network of casual friends who will support them, who will enjoy football games and meals with them. When we love people and spend time with them, they become much more open to hearing about the gospel. We can do this at fellowships or parties, but we need people with the gift of party to help us with the evangelistic and disciple-making process.

> *We need people with the gift of party to help us with the evangelistic and disciple-making process.*

Jesus recognized that people are more like sheep than eagles (Matthew 9:36). The implication is that most people prefer to run with the crowd than to fly alone. This is why the testimonial is so popular and effective in advertising. We are willing to go along with others simply because others are going along. Let me give you an example.

We all know about Marxism. Most Americans are opposed to Marxism. Yet who among us has studied its tenets well enough to say we have given Marxism an honest consideration? We simply reject it out of hand. I have never given Marxism careful consideration with a view to adopting its tenets. I will bet you haven't either. It is easy because most of us don't know any Marxists anyway.

Likewise, most of us know something of the Hindu faith. We know it exists and that millions of people have embraced it. Yet we have not seriously considered becoming Hindus. Why? One reason is that most of us don't know any Hindus.

Perhaps Mormonism provides a better example. Suppose you were to move to Salt Lake City. Everyone you work with is Mormon; your neighbors, Mormons. The people on your softball team and your closest friends—also Mormons. Then, to your surprise, your entire family converts to Mormonism. Don't you think you would probably look at Mormonism in a new light? For the first time in your life, you would probably give Mormonism some serious thought, wouldn't you?

I would. If my family and friends were Mormon, I would think about Mormonism as never before. Why? Because we're all influenced by the beliefs of our friends. Most people are followers. They like to believe what their friends and families believe.

> *People are more likely to become Christians if they don't have to cross racial, linguistic, or social barriers to do so.*

What does all this mean for evangelism and church growth? Everything. The key to fulfilling the Great Commission is to cross the social barrier before we try to cross the theological barrier. If we would consider Mormonism if *our* friends were Mormon, we can surmise that non-Christians will consider Christianity if we become *their* friends. People are more likely to become Christians if they don't have to cross racial, linguistic, or social barriers to do so.

Many of us have been trained to articulate our faith clearly and effectively. We can explain the gospel, and that is good. But non-Christians will probably never hear those words until a friend speaks them. We must love people before we expect them to come to love our Lord. If we want people to believe that God loves and accepts them, we must love and accept them.

In practical terms, this means spending time with people. It means inviting them into our homes and going out to dinner with them. We party with the people we love. We will work with anyone, but we spend casual time only with the people we care about. The greatest gift we can give someone is ourselves and our time. If we were half as effective at crossing social barriers as we have been at crossing theological barriers, we would have won the world years ago. One reason we haven't reached our country and our communities for Christ is that we simply do not love them. If we loved them, they would come. But they will not cross the barriers; we must go to them. Note that Jesus tells us to "*go* and make disciples" (Matthew 28:19).[4] We must take the initiative. We must do the going.

I used to think the problem was that we as class members simply didn't know enough "pre-Christians." That's certainly true of me. I can count on one hand the number of relationships I have with non-Christians. However, it is not true of most Christians. The members of my class each had five or more friends who were not Christians. But they weren't inviting these friends to Sunday school or to class parties. We are not reaching out to people with love, much less with the gospel.

In addition, two out of every one hundred people who attend a worship service are visitors and are great candidates for inviting. This is true of most churches. I consulted with a church recently in which four in one hundred were visitors. Yet the church was not growing. Why? Simple. We are not loving these visitors. We are not welcoming them into our homes. We are not inviting them to our parties. The greatest unmet need is love. The problem is not that we do not know anyone to love or to invite. We have plenty of people to invite. We simply are not doing it.

There is a good reason we aren't. We believe we need to invite people to the class itself. If we would double our classes every two years or less, we need to quit thinking so much about inviting people to class. We need to think, rather, about inviting people to monthly fellowships. Let me explain what I mean.

Suppose you take on the role of class outreach-leader. You are motivated, so you take a list of people who have visited the church recently and invite them to class. No one comes. You call again. Again, they stay away. You send a card. Nothing. You even visit and then call a third time. Still no response. This is church life in the trenches. This is how it really is. I know. I have been there and done that.

How do you think you would feel after all this? My best guess is, "awkward, painfully awkward." And if you are normal, you'll do anything to keep from feeling that way again. So you stop calling, stop inviting. Unfortunately, this happens every week in 320,000 churches across America. Christians begin to feel awkward about having their invitations to class or to church turned down, so they stop inviting.

What I suggest is that you stop inviting people to class. Quit inviting them to church. Invite them to a

> *If we can get them to the party, we cannot keep them away from the class.*

65

party instead. Ask them to go bowling. Invite them to go out for dinner. Get them on the softball team. What I have discovered is that if we can get them to the party, we cannot keep them away from class.

Here is how God taught me this. Our group needed a bridge to carry the gospel to our friends. People in our group knew outsiders, and we had recent visitors who were prospects, but neither group was responding to our invitations to attend class. We needed a way to reach them.

> *If you make people a part of the life of the group, you will not be able to keep them away from the Bible study.*

Then our group stumbled onto something accidentally. I hadn't read it in any book—it just seemed the thing to do. We started asking people to invite their friends to our fellowships. We asked them to bring them to play volleyball and to go to the beach with us. (In New Mexico, we have a beach but no ocean. It's called White Sands.) Then we recorded their names and invited them to the next event. We took a fairly systematic approach to this. We invited every visitor, whether or not that person was a prospect for our class or for the class down the hall. In our church, we encouraged free and open competition between classes. And, of course, we invited our own friends. Know what? They came! We found the bridge and discovered an important principle. If you make people a part of the life of the group, you will not be able to keep them away from the Bible study. After this, I rarely invited people to come to Bible study. But once they became part of the group and saw it as "us" instead of "them," their attendance was not a problem.

Why? Because we were meeting a basic human need. We were showing people genuine love and concern. That is not to say that all the people we invited came every time. Quite the contrary. Many of them didn't come, but enough did to make it worth our while. Every salesperson knows that you won't close on every call. The key is to make lots of calls. Furthermore, we offended very few people. People are often offended by telemarketing or uninvited visits at their door. But no one is offended by an invitation to a party. People love to be invited.

This is what you can expect to happen. You invite a couple to a Valentine's Day dinner, a bowling party, and a trip to a water park. Not interested. Later you invite them to play cards, and they come. They like playing cards. The door opens just a crack. Next time it is ten times easier for them to come. It is also ten times more likely that they will come to class and be exposed to halfway decent teaching. Why? Because they are coming to a group they already know. They turn you down for several more events. Then they come again. Then you invite them into your home. Then a member of your class does. Then another. Soon they have a whole group of friends who have all placed their faith in Christ. For the first time in their lives they must consider Christianity seriously.

There are a lot of bored and lonely people out there who are hungry for friendship. Fortunately, that is something we have. It is part and parcel of the gospel. All we need to do is widen our circle—intentionally. Every time my wife and I invite people into our home, I ask myself, "Is this something to which I could invite an outsider or a newcomer?" Often it's not, and that's OK. You do not have to invite outsiders to everything. You can have parties just for your Christian friends. But if you want to double your class every two years or less, invite non-Christians to be a part of your life on a regular basis.

> *There are a lot of bored and lonely people out there who are hungry for friendship.*

If we don't include people in our day-to-day lives, we will probably lose them from the church. A salesman stopped me in the mall the other day and asked, "You work at Calvary, don't you?" I didn't recognize him, but I smiled and said yes. Fortunately, he let me off the hook, "Oh, I don't expect you to recognize me. I don't attend Calvary any longer." We talked about business. I asked him about the software he was selling; he answered as any salesman might. Then he shocked me. "Do you know why I don't go to church [presumably any church] any longer?" "No," I replied, "but I'd really like to know." "Because people are friendly to you only at church."

His words cut like a knife. We must do better than that. That is not what it means to be a church. If we don't do any better than that, we don't deserve to be called a church. We must be friends to people inside and out-side the church building. That is what being the body of Christ is all about.

Please note that I am not asking you to give up a night you do not have. I'm not talking about altering a busy schedule to try to fit in one more thing. Rather, I'm talking about including non-Christians in your present lifestyle. When Jesus called the disciples, he called them to be *with him* (Mark 3:14). If you aspire to make disciples, you must invite people to be with you. Love them. Include them. Hang out with them. Our group reduced it to a formula: Invite every member and every prospect to every fellowship every month. "Every member"—that is a matter of inreach. It is developing quality relationships and loving each other. "Every prospect"—that is outreach. It is the stuff of the Great Commission.

> *Our group reduced it to a formula: Invite every member and every prospect to every fellowship every month.*

The same dynamic of awkwardness that I described earlier with reference to prospects is also true of absentees. One reason most churches have about half of their members gone every week is that it becomes awkward to invite them back. If they miss once, we may send a card. If they miss a second time, we may call. We may even pay them a visit (although this would be rare). But before long, if we keep calling, keep inviting them back to class, and keep saying, "We miss you," it becomes awkward for both sides. So we quit. It feels like obedience to the golden rule to stop inviting them. However, we can invite people to a fellowship every month until Jesus returns, and they'll always appreciate the invitation, as long as we don't pressure them or make them feel guilty about turning us down. It won't be awkward, even if they don't attend. And when their situation changes and the Spirit of God begins to woo them back, they will know the door is open for them to come back.

When we have had good friends who wandered from the faith for a season, we always tried to keep up with them on an informal, friendly basis. We would have breakfast about once a quarter. It was a little awkward because they had been so active in church life and now they weren't. It was difficult not to be judgmental, and I knew that, on some level, they, too, felt bad. Still, we kept doing it, and eventually the "Hound of heaven" chased them down. Tragedy came their way, and we were the ones they turned to. I was so glad we had been there during the dark years. That is what the body of Christ is to be to one another (see Galatians 6:1).

With how many people can you maintain this kind of personal involvement? Not very many, so we need all hands on deck. We need everyone involved in the business of loving people, every member a minister. We say this quite a bit, but we often fail to explain what it means. It means everyone loving someone. A minister loves and cares for the flock. This is life and friendship we're talking about. It's not a program; it's a way of living. It is loving one another. It is what it means to be the body of Christ. Everyone needs to be loved this way, because we are all capable of falling. Everyone needs to be loved, and it will take everyone loving to get the job done.

> *This is life and friend-ship we're talking about. It's not a program; it's a way of living.*

You may be wondering what kind of fellowship events to have. Before I give you the short list, remember this: Whatever you do the first three times won't be all that much fun. After that, just about anything will be fun. The reason is simple. This is not about bowling or miniature golf or swimming. It's about being together. People who love to be together don't really care what they do. People who don't love each other feel a little uncomfortable no matter what they do. OK, here is a short list of fun things to do: bowling, going out to eat, Valentine's Day parties (dinners are nice), miniature golf, Memorial Day picnics, swimming, potlucks, New Year's Eve parties (with lots of snacks), eating, Fourth of July parties, Super Bowl parties (Will your church let you out of church on Sunday night to do outreach?), great pumpkin chases, picnics, volleyball, Christmas parties, game nights, going to the beach, and eating. An easy way to plan a year of parties is to supplement seasonal events—

> *Whatever you do the first three times won't be all that much fun. After that, just about anything will be fun.*

Christmas, New Year's Eve, Valentine's Day, Memorial Day, and so on—with generic events such as bowling and miniature golf.

According to Dick Murray, it is a myth that most adults attend Sunday school primarily to learn. People attend for the fellowship, for the friends, for the life.[5] I dare you to invite every member and every prospect to every fellowship every month and then come back in two years and tell me your class didn't double.

NOTES

[1] Donald A. McGavran, *Understanding Church Growth* (Grand Rapids, MI: William B. Eerdmans Publishing Company, 1970), 223.

[2] Juan Carlos Ortiz, *Disciple* (Carol Stream, IL: Creation House, 1975), 58.

[3] The Greek word that most English Bibles translate "fellowship" means "to share or have things in common." People have an innate desire to share their lives with and have things in common with other people. In short, they long for fellowship.

[4] I have heard a number of explanations that take this "go" out of the Great Commission.

However, my Greek professor, Dr. Curtis Vaughan, explains, "Although the only imperative in the verse is the word for 'make disciples' [one word in the Greek], the other participles derive imperative force from the main verb. It is, therefore, proper to translate this as most English Bibles do: 'Go, make disciples.'" See also Maximilian Zerwick, *Biblical Greek* (Rome: Scripta Pontificii Instituti Biblici, 1963), § 373; H.E. Dana and Julius R. Mantey, *A Manual Grammar of the Greek New Testament* (New York, NY: Macmillan, 1927), § 201.10.

[5] Dick Murray, *Strengthening the Adult Sunday School Class* (Nashville, TN: Abingdon, 1981), 26.

The Anatomy of a Party

In this chapter we'll explore piece by piece what happens in a good party and how it affects guests, inactive members, and regular participants. Ultimately, we are learning how to use parties for God, as Levi did: "Then Levi held a great banquet for Jesus at his house, and a large crowd of tax collectors and others were eating with them" (Luke 5:29). Levi used a party for God, and we need to learn to do so as well.

A party has three parts: a beginning, a middle, and an end. We will examine the makeup and purpose of each of these in detail. The dynamics of parties also change from the first to the second to the third parties, and we will explore these changing dynamics as well.

At the end of the party, people sit around in little groups and talk. They talk about the weather, sports, politics, families, and—on occasion—religion. Sometimes they talk about important things, but mostly they just make small talk. This part of a party usually takes care of itself. Newcomers feel comfortable during this part of the party because they have built up some rapport with group members during the middle or activity part of the party.

The activity takes place during the middle part of the party. It may involve bowling, eating, picnicking, or playing silly games that the party people dreamed up to "draw us out." (Party people feel a need to draw us out, which is a euphemism for "embarrass us.") It may even be something special such as a baseball game or spending the day in the mountains. Obviously, it needs to be something that a newcomer can walk in off the street and participate in. For example, don't use bridge as a "bridge" to outsiders unless you know they're avid bridge players.

Like the small talk at the end of the party, the activity part usually takes care of itself. Newcomers generally feel the most comfortable during this part of the party because they know what's expected of them. They find comfort within the boundaries of the rules of the activity.

It is the early part of the party that can make or break your outreach ministry. When outsiders reach deep down and gather the courage to come to a strange place to meet a lot of strange people, when they risk a wasted or even horribly uncomfortable evening—someone had better be there to roll out the red carpet, to smile, to shake their hands, to effectively make small talk with them, and to comfortably introduce them to the group. If this doesn't happen, the last state will be worse—I mean much worse—than the first. It is a terrible mistake to invite people over and not be nice to them. It can cause much more harm than good.

> *It is a terrible mistake to invite people over and not be nice to them.*

If you remember people who came into your home or attended your Sunday school parties but who never came back, read the rest of this chapter carefully. I want to explain in detail what it means to roll out the red carpet for newcomers at a party. Doing these things effectively can spell the difference between effective outreach and a failed attempt at outreach that actually drives people away. There really is no middle ground. But before I get into the fine print, let me explain the differences between the first, second, and third parties. Different dynamics are at work when a newcomer comes to a second or a third party. I want to briefly address these.

Obviously, the easiest conversations are those that take place after newcomers are no longer newcomers. After people attend three or more parties, everything begins to become easy. You know enough about each other to carry on normal conversations. You are beginning to become friends. Their names are probably on the back of several members' phone books.

The first party that a newcomer attends is the second most comfortable. When you know nothing about a person, it's easy to ask lots of questions, if you only know how and are willing to do so. We will discuss that shortly.

By far and away the most difficult parties are the second and third parties. At these parties, you know the newcomers too well to ask the stereotypical newcomer-questions but not well enough to talk as friends. Friends tend to talk about more personal things, and they tend not to mind boring people with very mundane things. They talk about the garbage bag ripping on the way to the curb and other of life's little problems. We all need friends we can tell about the garbage bag ripping. Much of life is pretty mundane. Boring though it may be, we want and need to talk about it.

But we don't talk about these things with people we don't know very well. We're sensitive to the fact that these mundane things can be a bit boring and that many people really don't want to hear about the day-to-day details of our lives.

Similarly, we want and need to talk about our depression and our rebellious teenagers. But we don't talk about these things with just anyone. They are too personal.

The problem with the second and third parties is that we've already asked all the public-information questions such as "How long have you lived here?" and "Where do you work?" but we don't know if we're ready to talk about the mundane matters or personal things. The answer to this is pretty simple. Stay away from overly personal things, but dive into the mundane matters. It is an act of love. I may feel smothered if you ask about something too personal, but I'll probably be flattered if you ask me to explain exactly what I do from nine to five, what hobbies I pursue during my free time, or how I got into my present line of work. So, during the second and third parties, ask for a lot of details, and don't be afraid to re-inquire about the basics.

As you plan fellowships and invite people into your group, be sensitive to the fact that the second and third parties they attend will be the most awkward and will require the most care. If you asked about someone's work once but forgot, ask again. Don't forget a second time, however, and if you do, fake it. Telling people you've forgotten twice is admitting that they are really not very important to you. Just talk about something else, or say something like "Tell me what happens in a typical day for you from the time you get to work until you get home." Just hope someone doesn't answer, "Oh, I work at home. Remember? We talked about that last time." It's best to remember. Write it down if you have to.

Having briefly explored the dynamics of the second and third parties, let's now get into the specifics of how to make a party an effective outreach tool. Here is an outline for what needs to happen:

P lanning and preparation

A ctivity

R apport

T alk

Y uk! Yuk! Yuk!

Planning and preparation

Planning is the key to successful parties. Preparation is the implementation of the plan. Parties don't just happen. Someone must make them happen. Someone must talk about whether this prospect would be more comfortable visiting a home or going to a restaurant. Someone needs to think about matters such as

● what everyone will wear. (Is there a chance our guests might come overdressed or underdressed? How will they know what to wear?)

● what everyone will eat. (Everyone feels more comfortable with a handful of chips in one hand and a Diet Coke in the other.)

● how they will feel as they walk in the door. (Who will greet them? What will the first five minutes feel like for them?)

● what to do with the kids. (What if they bring their kids? How will they feel if we tell them not to bring their kids?)

● how to respond if they order something stronger than a Diet Coke with their meal.

Planning is the key to successful parties.

● how they will feel participating in the planned activity.

Planning effective parties is hard work. It requires turning on your brain and thinking about how it will feel to someone who has never before attended a church fellowship. If you haven't been a newcomer in a social setting recently, you might try it so you can acquaint yourself with how it feels. Visiting someone else's party is a good way to become sensitive to planning parties that newcomers will feel comfortable attending. Planning is the key to making it all happen.

All good ideas degenerate into work.

But planning isn't all that is needed. Preparation is the work. Sooner or later, all good ideas degenerate into work. We must plan our work and work our plan. Someone must buy the Diet Coke, make the coffeecake, and arrange for the baby sitter. Work—nothing more; never less. There's a reason Paul warned us not to become weary in doing good (Galatians 6:9). The ministry of loving people can weary the best of us.

Finally, this work needs to be done in a timely way so you are not rushing around at the last minute getting things ready. You need to spend the last minute preparing your mind to greet your guests.

Activity

Activities need to be planned and executed with newcomers in mind. If you are going out to eat, you need to consider whether they can afford the restaurant you have in mind. You may also want to be sensitive to the fact that not everyone likes Chinese food. Select a neutral restaurant. Similarly, choose activities that don't require previous experience. Bridge may not be a wise choice. The more a game coaxes people out of their shells and gets them laughing, the better. Charades works well, as do costume parties.

Whatever else you do, make sure that the party is a positive experience. There's nothing worse than being bored or offended at a party when you're supposed to be having fun. Break down the walls, and invite people to have fun.

Rapport

The ultimate test of the activity is the rapport that it creates. Rapport is that sense of having something in common. The goal of the party is that sometime during the evening the newcomers will say to themselves, "Ahhh, these are my kind of people. I feel at home here. I feel accepted here. I could get used to this."

People like to be with people with whom they have something in common. Engineers like to hang out with people who carry more than three pens and pencils, musicians with people who can tell the difference between a synthesizer and a piano. Life is complex enough that we can find something in common with almost anyone... if we work at it.

The goal of the party is that sometime during the evening the newcomers will say to themselves, "Ahhh, these are my kind of people. I feel at home here."

This is what fellowship is all about. The Greek word *koinōnia*, translated "fellowship" in most Bibles, means "to share or have in common." Theologically, it refers to a common faith, a common Lord, a common baptism. But *koinōnia*, like many words in the Bible, wasn't a theological word until the biblical writers made it one. It was originally just the common word for "common."

The human heart hungers to have something in common with others. The goal of a party is to give our guests the gift of feeling that they've met people with whom they have something in common.

Talk

> *People put up with work all week so they can go to a party on the weekend. And when they get to the party, they gather in clusters of four to six and talk.*

The way we establish rapport is through talking. Ever look at a party closely? People stand around in groups of four to six and talk. People put up with work all week so they can go to a party on the weekend. And when they get to the party, they gather in clusters of four to six and talk. Humans find this very pleasurable. The humans soul longs to be in communication. We long to talk. We love to talk.

These clusters of four to six form naturally at almost any kind of party, whether Christian or secular. They form in business parties as well as in church parties. People don't have to be told to do this. It just happens naturally. People like to gather in small groups and talk.

But what if a couple walks into a party and everyone else is already in a cluster of four to six engaging in this very pleasurable experience of talking? What if no small group invites them to join? This is an uncomfortable and painful experience for most people. They associate it with rejection. They feel like outcasts. They do not feel welcome. They do not feel loved. They want to leave, but they are too embarrassed to walk out.

How does it feel to attend a party when you're on the outside of all these clusters looking in? It feels awful—that's how it feels. Maybe it shouldn't feel awful. Maybe newcomers should just walk up to one of those clusters and say, "Hey, I want to be included. I want to share my stories and listen to yours. I want to be accepted."

Maybe. Maybe people shouldn't just stand on the outside, hoping someone will invite them in. Maybe they should be more brave. But they won't. They'll stand off to one side, feeling awful, until someone invites them in. They will stand on the outside of all those clusters and wish that someone would invite them in. They will stand there and think all kinds of bad thoughts about everyone there for inviting them to the party but not including them in one of the clusters. They will stand there and feel hurt and offended and angry. And if nothing changes, they will leave early. And they will never come back to that group's party again. They will probably never come back to the group or to that church again. They may give up on church altogether. They may even get a bad taste in their mouth about God. A lot depends on whether or not people are invited into those little clusters of four to six.

If people are included, they will start to feel good about the group. They will stand in one of the clusters just listening. After a while, they'll begin to feel comfortable and will say something. As time goes on, they will begin to feel good about the group. They'll start to feel loved and accepted. They will learn our names and our occupations and all about our kids. If all goes well, they will come to love our Lord and become his disciples. But first, we must invite them into our small groups. A lot depends on whether or not people are invited into those little clusters of four to six.

> *A lot depends on whether or not people are invited into those little clusters of four to six.*

When we invite people into our clusters, one other thing needs to happen. Often the conversation will roll along, and then there will be a little lull. Or, when the newcomers first walk up, there will be a brief pause. When this happens, someone must take the initiative to ask some questions without sounding as though the newcomers are being interrogated. Ask questions such as

- "Is this your first contact with the church?"
- "How long have you lived here?" (Be sure to avoid implying that something is wrong if they've lived in this town for a while and not attended a church.)
- "Where are you from originally?" (Whatever "originally" means. This question can open up the conversation to talking about a good deal of their life histories.)
- "Where do you work?"
- "What do you like to do for fun?"
- "Do you have any kids? How old are they? Where do they go to school? Are they on a soccer team?"

As you ask these questions, one of two things will happen. The newcomers will mention something you know something about, or the newcomers will bring up something you know nothing about. One of these two has to happen, and when it does, you have an opening for a whole series of follow-up questions.

If someone brings up a topic you know something about, talk about it. Suppose you share the same hometown or you both love fishing or she works where your brother works—follow it up. If you discover you grew up in the same small town, say, "Oh, really? Did you have Coach

Clod for shop? Did you really? What part of town did you live in? You're kidding! Small world." As you say this, something inside the newcomer will begin to relax. An instant rapport develops when we discover we have something in common with someone else. This is what we do if someone brings up a topic we know something about.

| *The easiest thing in the world is talking about something you don't know a thing about.* | If a newcomer mentions something we know nothing about, we follow a different tactic. We become investigative reporters. The easiest thing in the world is talking about something you don't know a thing about. Just listen to people—they do it all the time. Suppose he says he's a firefighter. You've never known a firefighter, so you immediately become an investigative reporter: "A firefighter—wow. I've never met a firefighter before. |

How often do you go out on calls? Have you ever been in a really dangerous situation when you thought you might die? How do you spend your time between fires? What kind of hours do you work? How did you get into firefighting? What kind of training is required? Do you think you are in it for the long haul? That's really interesting."

Most people love to talk about themselves, but sensitivity and caution are always in order. Some people are private, so we need to be careful not to act too much like investigative reporters. People don't want to be interrogated. There's a difference between showing interest and interrogating. Be sensitive to that point when people have shared all they care to share.

Good conversationalists will reciprocate and ask you similar questions. This is the birth of engaging, evenhanded, enjoyable conversation. Everyone in the group talks about the same amount of time. You discuss various topics of interest. No one dominates; no one is excluded. This is group life at its best, and it can happen with perfect strangers. Many times, however, the people we are trying to reach are less-than-perfect conversationalists.

Sometimes people love talking about themselves so much that they let you do all the asking. You ask about their work, their kids, their hobbies, and their background, and it never occurs to them to ask you anything. This may be either out of sheer selfishness or a more benign shyness. In either case, you're left doing all the asking while they're left doing all the answering. What do you do? Do you just keep asking questions and let them keep babbling on about themselves? Or do you dive in at some point and say, "We've been talking about you quite awhile. Now let's talk about me a little"? The second option is exactly what you should do.

Obviously, you don't need to be so blunt; there are nicer ways to make the transition from talking about them to talking about you. But it needs to be done. Some people simply don't have the stuff of conversational skill. This may be why they need someone to befriend them. They probably need a friend who will walk into their lives, ask questions, listen to their answers, and say, "Let's talk about *me* for a while." Not that you actually say that. You simply break in and talk about yourself a bit. Don't overdo it; just even things out a bit. They want to know about you; that is why they came. They just don't know how to ask.

Conversation is a skill: the skill of being curious, the skill of asking questions, the skill of listening. It's the skill of empathizing, of saying, "Gosh, that must have been awful." But it is also the skill of talking, of telling stories, and of monitoring the conversation so that everyone participates in a balanced way. Finally, conversation is also the skill of humor. This is conversation at its best. When one of those clusters of four to six begins laughing until they roll on the floor, the other groups will point and ask, "What's with them?" But secretly, they'll wish they had sat at a table where the laughter was boiling over.

Yuk! Yuk! Yuk!

Friendships are born in laughter. Tears—yes, we must endure those, but laughter—we crave laughter. Friends laugh together. We work with anyone, but we laugh with the people we love. Laughter: that natural intoxication from heaven, that state in which we lose ourselves in joy. We are never happier than when we hold our sides and squint until we cry in laughter.

> *We are never happier than when we hold our sides and squint until we cry in laughter.*

Laughter cannot be programmed. We cannot put on the agenda of the party, "We will all laugh at nine o'clock." I wish we could, but laughter will not be summoned that way. Laughter comes when it wishes. We may only welcome it or bid it leave. We cannot constrain it to come at will.

Some are tempted to check laughter at the door. Perhaps they think they are too dignified to laugh, that laughter is beneath them. Don't be one of them. If God grants your group the gift of laughter, throw open your arms and embrace it. Laughter is a precious gift, a welcome guest. This is life at its best—to laugh with our friends.

There are limits, of course, situations in which laughter is inappropriate and God's gracious gift becomes a curse in our hands. The first is laughter at the expense of someone's self-esteem. Much of the world's laughter is like this. It is laughter that puts down, laughter that scorns, laughter that laughs at. This is sin and should be avoided at all costs. "Oh, we were only kidding. He understands. We do it all the time." All the more reason to stop. Now. This kind of laughter gets old very quickly. The object of your laughter may be laughing the loudest on the outside, but on the inside he is crying as his soul is being crushed. Stop it. Laughing should never be laughing at.

The second perversion of laughter relates to our sexuality. I do not know what it is about humans that causes us to find sex so humorous, but we most certainly have a tendency in that direction. Comedians love to get a crowd laughing about sex because it is so easy. But the Bible warns us to have none of it: "Nor should there be obscenity, foolish talk, or coarse joking" (Ephesians 5:4).

With these two warnings in mind, let us drink deeply from the chalice of laughter. Let us welcome it, enjoy it. Let us be thankful to God for the gift of laughter.

Summary

There you have it—the anatomy of a party. There is a beginning, an activity, and an ending. The most important part is the beginning, when people stand around in clusters of four to six and talk. We need to look over our shoulders regularly to make sure everyone is in one of these clusters. It is awful on the outside. We need to develop the skills of conversation, asking questions and telling our own stories. And when God graces our group with laughter, we need to welcome it as a friend. God can use parties like this to change the world. God is looking for ordinary people with the gift of party to help with the evangelistic and disciple-making process.

The Most Receptive People in Town

One of the basic principles of church growth is that we should concentrate our efforts on receptive people. I was surprised to learn that we can predict who will be most receptive. For example, on average, people who have experienced change tend to be more receptive than those who have not. That is why people who have just moved, had a baby, or gone through a divorce are often unusually receptive to the gospel. All things being equal, it is wiser to concentrate on these people than on those who have not experienced change. It makes good sense to focus most of our efforts on the reachable.

> *On average, people who have experienced change tend to be more receptive than those who have not.*

Imagine that you head a missions agency. One country is open to the gospel; another is very resistant. If you had only one hundred missionaries, how many would you send to each area? Conventional church-growth thinking would send ninety-seven to the ripe area for the sake of the harvest and three to the unripe area just to monitor the situation.

Here's the rationale. Suppose you were a farmer with a huge orange orchard. The fruit is ripe in one field, and 90 percent of the oranges are ready to be harvested today. In another field, only 10 percent are ready to be harvested. If you had one hundred workers, how would you distribute them? Ninety-seven to the ripe field and three to the under-ripe field just to monitor the situation. Most of your resources would go toward picking the ripe fruit.

In light of this, you need to answer a very important question: Who are the most receptive people to your ministry and to that of your class? In other words, who should you concentrate 97 percent of your energy on?

> *Who are the most receptive people to your ministry and to that of your class?*

The first answer is: friends of your class members. Friends of your class members will tend to respond well to you, to your class, and to your approach to the gospel ministry. That is why you should encourage the members of your class to invite their friends to your parties. Friends of your class members are the most receptive people to you. But if they won't eat ice cream with you, it's not likely they will embrace your God. Work diligently at acquainting these people with real, live, flesh-and-blood disciples. They will be much more receptive to the gospel after they've met half a dozen committed Christians. If their names are scribbled on our phone books, it is likely they will come to love our Lord.

You should also concentrate your efforts on people who visit your church. Visitors are usually very responsive to the gospel, but most churches retain only a small percentage of them. I've consulted with some churches that were reaching no more than 10 percent of their visitors. People were walking into the showroom, kicking the tires, and walking out on foot. It makes good sense to place a major effort here. Concentrate your efforts on these receptive people.

There are several ways to reach these receptive groups with the gospel. You can invite every member and every prospect to every fellowship every month. You can also love them. The greatest of the two is love. If we love them, they will come. Concentrate these high-results strategies on the most receptive groups in town—the friends of your class members and the visitors of the church—and your class will double in two years or less.

Let me offer some good news. You don't have to adopt every idea in this book to double every two years. My guess is that you'll double your class in *less than a year* if you implement every idea I discuss. You may be a hard charger who wants to do that. But there may be things in the book that just don't fit your style. They don't fit who God made you to be. Can God use someone who doesn't like having people in his or her home? You bet! Can God use a person who hates calling on the phone? Easily! Can God use someone who doesn't like fellowships? Of course he can! Can God use a person who doesn't like to do any of those things? You bet! God is a marvelously creative God, and it is his business where and how he uses you. Doubling your class is not about methods; it is about results. Any ethically sound, biblically allowable method that gets the job done is a good method. This seemed to be Paul's strategy:

> Though I am free and belong to no man, I make myself a slave to everyone, to win as many as possible. To the Jews I became like a Jew, to win the Jews. To those under the law I became like one under the law (though I myself am not under the law), so as to win those under the law. To those

not having the law I became like one not having the law (though I am not free from God's law but am under Christ's law), so as to win those not having the law. To the weak I became weak, to win the weak. I have become all things to all men so that by all possible means I might save some. I do all this for the sake of the gospel, that I may share in its blessings (1 Corinthians 9:19-23).

These methods have worked marvelously for me, and I believe they can work for you as well. But if they don't, try something else. Do whatever it takes to produce the desired results. I have heard too many people say, "We had a good year in our Sunday school this year. Enrollment is down. Attendance is down. Giving is down. But we had some good meetings. And we have such a sweet spirit." God called us to more than good meetings and a sweet spirit. He called us to make disciples.

To fill your class with disciples and double your class every two years or less, don't go after anyone and everyone. Concentrate your efforts on the most receptive people in town. Start by taking good care of the people on your class roll. Then seek out the people who visit your worship services, and get to know the friends of your class members. Finally, invite them all to a party at which you can show them God's love.

> *To fill your class with disciples and double your class every two years or less, don't go after anyone and everyone. Concentrate your efforts on the most receptive people in town.*

Zone Offense

The most receptive people in town are sitting right beneath our noses each and every week. The people most likely to respond to an invitation to discipleship are all around us. They are the people who worship with us each weekend but who do not attend Sunday school. In most churches, far more people attend a worship service than a Sunday school class. Disciples, however, are made in small groups.

If you want to put faces to the numbers, just sit at the back of your worship area and watch the people as they leave—as they walk out the door and across the parking lot, get into their cars, and go home. Touched by the truth but not changed, inoculated with a small dose of the gospel but not infected with the real disease, they may even think to themselves, "I got a little religion. I feel good about myself. That is all I need."

But Christianity was designed to be learned and lived out in community. There is no such thing as a disciple who is not in some sort of community. Many of the biblical commands are "one another" commands, things we are to do for and to and with each other. They simply cannot be done alone. They can only be obeyed in the context of relationships that form within a small group. Here are only a few of the verses that speak to this:[1]

● "Accept *one another*, then, just as Christ accepted you, in order to bring praise to God" (Romans 15:7).

● "I appeal to you, brothers, in the name of our Lord Jesus Christ, that all of you agree with *one another* so that there may be no divisions among you and that you may be perfectly united in mind and thought" (1 Corinthians 1:10).

● "You, my brothers, were called to be free. But do not use your freedom to indulge the sinful nature; rather, serve *one another* in love" (Galatians 5:13).

● "Be kind and compassionate to *one another*, forgiving each other, just as in Christ God forgave you" (Ephesians 4:32).

● "Therefore encourage *one another* and build each other up, just as in fact you are doing" (1 Thessalonians 5:11).

● "And let us consider how we may spur *one another* on toward love and good deeds" (Hebrews 10:24).

● "Dear friends, let us love *one another*, for love comes from God. Everyone who loves has been born of God and knows God" (1 John 4:7).

How can would-be disciples obey these commands if they come to church only to worship? How can they do these things without being part of a group? How can they benefit from encouragement, teaching, loving, and fellowship unless they are a part of a group? They

> *The life of the body is in the cell.*

can't—and they will never become disciples without these things. In fact, they may become inoculated against the gospel. The life of the body is in the cell.

I used to believe that many of these people were involved in home groups of some kind. Then we took a survey. We asked, "What kind of groups are you involved in?" Most did not belong to any group of any kind. It's probably true in your church as well.

It's true despite the fact that people are desperately lonely. Rick Warren writes: "We're experiencing an epidemic of loneliness in society. One Gallup poll reported that four in ten Americans admit to frequent feelings of 'intense loneliness.' Americans are, in fact, the loneliest people in the world."[2]

The question is, "What are we going to do about it?" One thing is certain: Public announcements will have little effect. Invitations from the pastor to attend a group will make little difference.

> *The concept of a zone offense is pretty simple. Assign class members to sit throughout the worship area: one person front left, another back left, one couple front center, another back center, and so on.*

I suggest that you set up a zone offense. The concept of a zone offense is pretty simple. Assign class members to sit throughout the worship area: one person front left, another back left, one couple front center, another back center, and so on. Class members are to sit in their assigned sections every week. In time, they will get to know the people who normally sit in those sections. They can observe whether they go to Sunday school. They can learn their names. And they can invite them to class or to a class party. (People are more likely to attend a fellowship before they visit class.) They can pray for them. They can be their first friends in class. They can invite them to their homes as an expression of hospitality.

If every class sets up a zone offense, you will have a

number of people in every service who are ministering in every section of the worship area. In time, you will get to know all those who attend worship but not a small group. More important, they will come to know individuals in the body. They'll begin to trust you, and you'll have an opportunity to invite them to dozens of things. Eventually, many of them will take the next step in the discipleship process.

You can double your class simply by making disciples out of people who might otherwise be inoculated against the gospel. I am speaking of the people who attend your worship services but who do not attend a group. You can double your class in two years or less simply by reaching out to them through a zone offense. They may be the most reachable people in your town.

NOTES

[1] See also Romans 12:10; 13:8; 15:14; 16:16; Ephesians 5:19, 21; Colossians 3:13, 16; Hebrews 3:13; 10:25; 1 Peter 1:22; 3:8; 4:9; 1 John 1:7; 3:11, 23; 4:11, 12; and 2 John 1:5.

[2] Rick Warren, *The Purpose Driven Church* (Grand Rapids, MI: Zondervan, 1995), 315.

The Law of 17
Large Numbers

I learned a great deal from my participation in Norm Whan's telemarketing campaign, "The Phone's for You." The campaign was a success, not so much because of what it accomplished or the people it reached (although it did some good and reached some people), but because it rocked me out of some traditional ways of thinking. It opened me up to the truth of the law of large numbers.

The law of large numbers is a law.

The law of large numbers is like the laws of aerodynamics and gravity. You can't break these laws; you can only learn to cooperate with them. You learn to live with them instead of in opposition to them. You learn to take advantage of them instead of being trapped by them.

The theme of this book is how to double your class in two years or less. If you're thinking only of counting noses, you can do it much faster than two years. I recently started teaching a new group that doubled in one week and then doubled the second week as well. We increased from five to nine to twenty. How did we do it? Well, halfway decent teaching for one. I also mailed out three hundred letters each week. I advertised the class in the church newsletter and bulletin, and I personally called one hundred people. (Calling is extremely effective.) The law of large numbers states that some of them will come. And it is a law.

Notice that it is the law of *large* numbers.

The law of large numbers applies in small groups and small churches but not to small numbers. What this means is that things even out over time. Suppose you discover that half the people you invite to your class respond positively and say they will come. Half of these actually come. Then you observe that only half the people who attend one time come back a second time, and only half of the people who attend two or more times enroll in your class. Finally, you notice that half the people who are enrolled are present on any given day.

Question: If the above percentages are right, how many people will you have to invite to increase your average attendance by one? Answer: thirty-two. Note the following chart:

32 people were called
16 say they will come
8 actually come
4 attend a second time
2 enroll in the class
1 is present on a given Sunday

I am *not* saying that this chart is true without exception. I'm not claiming that if you call two people one will promise to attend. It depends on who those people are. If they've visited your church, you will probably do better than one out of two. It also depends on what you invite them to. If you invite them to class, you probably won't average 50 percent. But if you invite them to your home for coffeecake and cards, you'll probably do better than one out of two. If you pick up the phone book and call people at random, you'll probably do much worse (about 2 percent or less).

Things even out over time.

But let's suppose that, on average, you need to make thirty-two calls to increase your attendance by one. What are the chances of making thirty-two calls (no more, no less) and increasing your attendance by one? The answer to that question is statistically more complex than my brain can comprehend. Suffice to say that it is less than 100 percent. Why? The law of large numbers. Things even out over time. What if you make 3,200 calls over a two-year period? What are the chances of increasing your attendance by one hundred? Very good. Why? The law of large numbers. Things even out over time.

You may lose some of the details of what I'm saying, but please do not miss the main point. You don't have to make 3,200 calls to double your class in two years. You can achieve very high percentages if you invite the right people (the most receptive ones) to the right events (coffeecake and Diet Coke in your home). But you will not reach them all.

Essentially, the law of large numbers states that things work out over time. The bottom line is: If you invite people to your home this week and no one shows up, try again next week. If only half the people you call are nice to you, stay with it. Suppose that you make three calls and all three are rude to you. What do you do? Stay with it. Why? The law of large numbers. Things even out over time. It *will* turn around. But what should you do if you call two hundred people and everyone is rude? Change your strategy. You have made enough calls that the law of large numbers is starting to take effect... and your strategy is obviously bad.

We once spent an entire summer knocking on people's doors in Farmington, New Mexico. Out of the two thousand doors our knuckles personally rapped, how many people do you think visited the church even one time?

Zero. I think it was time to change our strategy.

I'm not saying we should not knock on doors. I am saying that we should not knock on doors if knocking on doors does not work. I believe in direct mail, not because I am lazy, but because it works. It gets the desired results. We send out mail, and people visit. And when I ask them why they visited, they say, "I got this pamphlet in the mail." It works. Do whatever works.

But remember, you won't know if something will work until you really give it a decent try. That's what is meant by the law of large numbers.

However, the law of large numbers works both positively and negatively. A story is told of a man whose experience was similar to ours in Farmington. After knocking on two thousand doors and having no one respond, he resolved to knock on two thousand more the next summer. I think that is dumb, and the law of large numbers supports me. If you have knocked on two thousand doors and no one has responded, you have established a predictable ratio. If you choose to knock on more doors, change what you say. Change the area you are working in. Change something, but do not keep working the same tired method if it isn't working. That is not faithfulness. It is stupidity.

You've probably heard of missionaries who ministered fifty years for only one convert. Am I claiming that they were no more faithful than I? Not on your life. I really can't judge them. But if they used the same methods that worked in Peoria, never altering them

> *Don't confuse activity with productivity.*

even though the methods weren't working in another culture, maybe they could have worked smarter. But I really can't say. I am simply encouraging you to work smarter, not harder. Don't confuse activity with productivity. Do what works. And when you find something that works, do not be discouraged by three rude phone calls.

What works in the Saddleback Valley may not work in Atlanta. What works in South Barrington, Illinois, may not work in Dallas. By the same token, what works for young married adults may not work for young singles. That is why God has called you, a unique person, to do what works in your situation. Be creative. Be flexible. Experiment. Fail. And figure out in the process the best way to reach the people whom God places before you.

> *No cookie-cutter ministry, right out of a box, is going to work everywhere.*

No cookie-cutter ministry, right out of a box, is going to work everywhere. When machines are churned out of a factory, they are all alike. But when God creates, he does so creatively—one person, one ministry at a time. They are all unique. Look at a tree. It is balanced, but not symmetrical. That is how God creates.

You are God's expert in knowing how to reach, minister to, and care for the people in your area. No one knows as much about them as you do. Likewise, no one knows how to minister to your group as well as you do. Learn from everyone, but above all else, discover what God is doing in the world around you, and follow him. Part of how we find that out is to experiment. Work out a plan. Then work the plan.

You can double your class in two years or less by following God's creative plan for your life and for the life of your group. But whatever your plan, it will probably involve planting a lot of seeds to produce a reasonable number of mature plants. This is the law of the four soils, according to Matthew 13:1-23. Some seed fell here, some there. Most of them didn't produce . . . but some did. This is the law of large numbers.

What 623 Phone Calls Taught Me

I had to make 623 telephone calls to discover the lessons I'm going to give you here. All you have to do to learn them is read this chapter carefully.

The hard way is not necessarily the best way. In fact, the scales are often tilted in favor of the easiest way. Calling is much easier than visiting, and we need to make lots of calls on every level. We are busy. The people we need to contact are busy. If we can save them time, we do them a service and save ourselves time. There are times a phone call won't do, when only a visit will suffice. But this is pretty rare.

You will hear "no" much more often than you will hear "yes." This is the law of large numbers. I just devoted an entire chapter to the subject, but let me review: Most people you invite will not be interested in a given event. So if you want some people to show up, you have to ask a much bigger group than what you hope to attend.

Suppose your goal is to grow your church by a thousand. If you want to have a thousand new people attending, you must be willing to hear "no" an awful lot, maybe a million times. Out of the million you invite, one hundred thousand will show up once. Ten thousand of those will join. Out of those, eight thousand will move away within ten years, and out of the remaining two thousand, only half will be here on any given Sunday. If you want a thousand new people, simply invite a million. I wish I had a nickel for every time I've heard this: "If we can ever get them all to show up at the same time, we'll really have a big group here." True.

But they will all never show up at the same time. In our telemarketing campaign, we called nineteen thousand people. If all nineteen thousand had shown up, we would have had a pretty sizable group. But they didn't show up for us, and they won't come to your class either. That is, all of them won't come. Now the good news.

Some will come. This is the good news. Part of the price of growth is hearing "no" a number of times. How many times are you willing to hear "no" to get the job done? We had people calling the church months after our telemarketing campaign. One woman spoke

> *Part of the price of growth is hearing "no" a number of times.*

91

tearfully of an invitation she had received in the mail. After eleven invitations, we had finally gotten through. There is a crass side of me that wants to ask, "Where were you when the eleven other invitations arrived?" But I'm sure God would ask me, "What difference does it make? She's listening now." It wasn't until the twelfth contact, but with tears in her eyes, she thanked us: "I didn't know anyone cared." In time, she came to live the disciple's life and is still doing so today.

Multiple media will help get the message through. The larger the church, the more redundant the communication must be. A telemarketing campaign is two phone calls and five pieces of mail. You call once, send a bunch of mail, and then call again. Seven total contacts. This redundancy is effective. Telemarketing experts say that if you reduce the number of contacts to three or four instead of seven, your results will nose dive.

These days, calling by phone has an added benefit. If you call someone who isn't home but who has an answering machine, you can leave a message. Leaving a message accomplishes two things: You communicate the information you need, and you convey a personal touch. We receive official mail from all kinds of people, but friends call. For example, as I was writing this paragraph, our dermatologist called to tell us that a mole removed from my wife was benign. He wished me a happy New Year, answered a question about my son, and asked about my Christmas. Because of his call, I feel cared for as I would if he were an old-fashioned doctor who makes house calls. The phone is personal that way.

Finally, when you use the phone, be as conversational, friendly, and down-home as you can. Be casual. Talk—don't speak. "My wife and I were gonna have some friends over for some coffee, ice cream, and cards" is much better than, "This Friday night, there will be an informal gathering of three couples from our Sunday school class. You are cordially invited to attend."

Use three media to invite people: oral invitations during class, phone calls, and written invitations to everyone.

Summary

Invite every member and every prospect to every fellowship every month, but don't merely announce fellowships and parties in class. Use three media to invite people: oral invitations during class, phone calls, and written invitations to everyone. If you do this, you will double your class every two years or less.

Give Friday nights to Jesus.

An especially powerful kind of fellowship is giving Friday nights to Jesus. By this I mean inviting outsiders to an informal time of fellowship, coffeecake, Diet Coke, and cards. It is the most powerful strategy we have. People who are opposed to the gospel are not opposed to ice cream (or coffeecake).

Giving Friday
Nights to Jesus

Fasten your seat belt, friend, because this is the most high-powered approach we have. I do not know anything that works better than giving Friday nights to Jesus. Giving Friday nights to Jesus will reach more people in less time than any other method around. In fact, if you give Friday nights to Jesus and your class does not double in two years or less, it probably can't be done.

The truly remarkable part is that giving Friday nights to Jesus is more fun than Six Flags. You wouldn't think a ministry could be so effective and so much fun at the same time. But isn't it just like God to make something enjoyable and effective? Sometimes God makes it easy for us to "rejoice in the Lord always" (Philippians 4:4).

We didn't dream this ministry up—God sovereignly led us to it through the circumstances of our lives. And if I had not seen it in action, I may have never been convinced of its effectiveness. Here's how it works.

We used to have our friends over on Friday nights to play cards. We would play games, tell jokes, and enjoy dessert together. One day I suggested to my wife, Sharon, that we invite a couple who had visited the church to join us the next Friday. We did, and we had a good time in the process. During the entire evening, we never said a word about church, Sunday school, the Bible, or anything else remotely religious. Do you know what? They joined the church in a few weeks, and now he's teaching a class. And both would tell you that they were not living the disciple's life before they played cards and ate dessert with us that night.

A few weeks later, we invited another couple over. We played cards; we laughed; we ate dessert; we had a good time. Guess what? After a few weeks, they joined the church and became very active in the group. They, too, would tell you they were not living the disciple's life before we played cards with them.

After six months of this, I did a little research. I discovered that forty-five couples who would have been prospects for our class had visited the church during that time. We were able to have ten of these couples to our house to play cards. Nine out of the ten joined the church and became involved in the class. Out of the remaining thirty-five, only three had joined. I don't know of any method more effective in assimilating visitors than this hospitality ministry.

That is why I say, if you want to double your class every two years or less, give Friday nights to Jesus. Invite your friends over. Play cards. Tell jokes. Enjoy dessert.

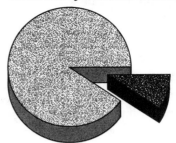

Ninety Percent of the People We Played Cards With Joined the Church

People who did join the church

People who did not join the church

Laugh. Have a good time. But most of all, include an outsider couple. Ministry has never been so much fun.

George Barna's research indicates that 7 percent of the people who do not attend church plan to do so within the next year.[1] If churches consistently gave Friday nights to Jesus, we could see 90 percent of those people stay. That is, at least 5 percent of the unchurched would come into the church each year. Another 33 percent of the unchurched are open to attending church, according to Barna. The most likely thing to attract them is the invitation of a friend.[2] So when they do come, we need to have a strategy to get them to stay. We need to become a Velcro church rather than a Teflon church. Rick Warren explains, "For your church to grow you must be *nice* to people when they show up!"[3]

"For your church to grow you must be nice *to people when they show up!"*

The best way to do that is to give Friday nights to Jesus.

This ministry is based on sound church-growth thinking: People are not interested in a friendly church; they are looking for friends.[4] That is what we were to the couples we invited to our house. We were friends to them, and they were friends to us. When we had our babies, they were at the hospital. They became our friends. William Hendricks discovered that people who leave the church often do so because they hunger for community. "They still dream of being a part of an intimate group of believers," he

People are not interested in a friendly church; they are looking for friends.

writes. "They want to share life together with a handful of others where they can know and be known."[5] Giving Friday nights to Jesus creates the kind of community that people long for.

Let me answer a couple of obvious questions. No, it does not have to be Friday night, and you do not have to play cards. You can take people out to lunch, go bowling, or play golf. You might go out to lunch with them after church. But do something fun. Do whatever you enjoy doing with your friends. But include some outsiders in your life, whether they're newcomers to the faith or believers who are new to town.

You might wonder how this ministry differs from inviting every member and every prospect to every fellowship every month. There is some overlap, at least as to function. However, there are also significant differences. The monthly fellowships are events that the entire class and all the prospects are invited to attend. Giving Friday nights to Jesus is a more informal get-together with a handful of friends. It is this informality and friendliness that give this approach its power. As soon as it becomes a big, formal affair, it is dead. It is the life of the body lived out in small groups, a life that outsiders are invited to join.

I used to teach a fourth-grade boys Sunday school class. Giving Friday nights to Jesus was effective for them—only I did it Tuesday afternoons. The most effective outreach I had with those kids had nothing to do with the class time. Every Tuesday afternoon I would take them out for a Coke. (This was before I discovered Diet Coke.) I listened to them and tried to get into their world. This, too, is an example of giving Friday nights to Jesus. Not surprisingly, some of these boys placed their faith in Christ.

Some churches provide a budget for the pastor to take people to lunch. This is another example of giving Friday nights to Jesus. It is also one of the best investments a church can make. Granted, it costs money, but the souls are worth it. I suspect that 90 percent of the people for whom we buy pizza will move on in the disciple-making process. Besides, the average family of four who attends our church regularly gives two thousand dollars a year, so the dinner budget is well worth it. It's also based on a biblical principle: "Cast your bread upon the waters, for after many days you will find it again" (Ecclesiastes 11:1).

The hard work of having fun

Don't get the idea that this is all fun and games. It's not. It's hard work to have fun. And when you give Friday nights to Jesus, someone has to make the coffeecake and buy the Diet Coke. Someone has to vacuum the floor and clean the kitchen. Someone has to call the guests and friends. As I said earlier, every good idea degenerates into work.

> *Every good idea degenerates into work.*

Planning fun is the easy part. Getting ready for the fun is work, hard work that needs to be shared. So let me say a word to the husbands and wives reading this: Don't make your spouse do all the work. Getting ready for the party is too much work for one person to do it all.

Peter commands us, "Offer hospitality to one another without grumbling" (1 Peter 4:9). Sometimes people will come to your house and, after their rowdy kids tear up your playroom, will not offer to clean it up. Offer hospitality without grumbling. Sometimes you will invite people over, and they will promise to come and then not show up. Offer hospitality without grumbling. Sometimes people will be social bores, obnoxious, or rude. Offer hospitality without grumbling.

One time we had four couples lined up to come over and play cards. None of them showed up. I got mad. I was disobedient to the command not to grumble. I angrily called one of them on the phone and asked, "Where are you? Why aren't you here?" I really let him have it. He joined the church anyway and has since become a deacon and a Sunday school teacher. But that is only because of the grace of God.

The Bible *commands* us, "Get into the habit of inviting guests home for dinner" (Romans 12:13, The Living Bible). If we will simply do what this command says, we will see tremendous fruit. That is what it all comes down to, doesn't it? Simply obeying what God has called us to do. It is amazing how much of church growth boils down to doing what God has already told us to do. You can double your class in two years or less if you and your group will give Friday nights to Jesus.

NOTES

[1] George Barna, *Evangelism That Works* (Ventura, CA: Regal Books, 1995), 68.

[2] Barna, *Evangelism That Works*, 70.

[3] Rick Warren, *The Purpose Driven Church* (Grand Rapids, MI: Zondervan, 1995), 210.

[4] Warren, *The Purpose Driven Church*, 312.

[5] William D. Hendricks, *Exit Interviews* (Chicago, IL: Moody Press, 1993), 260.

Group Life:
Get Serious About
Having Fun

The other night I sat with two of our singles, Greg Powe and Dan Orth, at a banquet. During the course of the evening, they asked a question that always makes me uneasy: "What classes do you have for new believers?" After explaining some of the things we've had in the past, I admitted that right now we do not have any classes per se for new Christians.

Later, as I reflected on this question, I realized that I've made a 180-degree change on this issue. I used to think that new Christians need a good deal of content so they can be "rooted and built up in him, strengthened in the faith...and overflowing with thankfulness."[1] I thought we should teach new Christians how to have assurance of salvation, victory over sin, and power in prayer. We thought we needed to help them discover how to use their spiritual gifts, have quiet time, study the Bible, memorize Scripture, and spend a day in prayer. All these things are important, and we should probably be doing better than we are at teaching them. But I now contend that there is something more important than all of them.

Unfortunately, I learned this lesson the hard way. A young lady had been faithfully attending class for six months or more. Then she became ill and spent three weeks in the hospital. She was home recovering for another six weeks. And in all this time, no one went to see her. No one called. There were no messages on her answering machine when she got home, no cards in the mailbox. And worst of all, when she came back, no one even noticed she had been gone. No one acknowledged her absence; no one told her she had been missed. In fact, no one had missed her. When we behave like that, we don't deserve to be called a church. We are something far worse.

The solution, of course, is to set up a computer program that will contact absentees automatically. Simply scan in the bar code that represents the absent person's name, and have the database spit out a letter, a fax, and an e-mail.

NO!

The solution is love, connection. What we need is to have this young lady's name scribbled on the back of half a dozen members' phone books. What we need is for someone to love her. You see, when I say, "We reduced it to a formula: Invite every member and every prospect to every fellowship every month," don't take this idea of a formula too literally. The formula is an expression of love. It is getting intentional about love. Really caring about people is what matters.

Do you know what happens when people are not missed? They miss. People who miss and are not missed, miss. If we do not have new people's names on the back of half a dozen phone books, poking some good content inside of them will not help.

> *People who miss and are not missed, miss.*

This is what I have discovered. If you assimilate people into a group, they will learn the content (assuming, of course, the teacher is doing a halfway decent job each and every week). In time, they'll learn how to have a quiet time, how to overcome sins they struggle with, how to get along with others, and how to use their spiritual gifts. Even if they receive limited content in class, they'll learn something from the sermons...if they stay around long enough. But in order for them to stay around, someone must love them. And in order for you to have people to teach, you must assimilate them into the group. They have to know that you care before they care what you know.

This is why I say: Get serious about having fun. If you're not having fun with your class, they won't be having fun with you. Have fun with your group. Great teachers get together with their class members during the week almost every week.

How do you know when you've succeeded? When class members are really good friends with each other as well as with you. When you see them walking slowly down the hall, swapping stories about last week's activities and making arrangements to get together next week. That is what you are trying to create. If new believers make seven friends in your group, they will never leave. When their names are scribbled on the back of seven people's phone books, they are well on their way to becoming disciples. But if you don't assimilate them, all the theology of Martin Luther, John Calvin, Jonathan Edwards, and Charles Spurgeon will not keep them.

> *If new believers make seven friends in your group, they will never leave.*

Let me add a closing word about spiritual gifts. We understand a great deal about gifts such as teaching, leadership, and mercy. We need, however, to understand and recognize the gift of party (a k a hospitality). Some of you reading this book have the gift of party, and no one ever told you that you have it or that there even is such a thing. Consequently, the entire body has been robbed of your gift and your ministry. If I were in your church, I would ask you to stand so I could talk to you directly. (People who have the gift of party are normally extroverts who don't mind being singled out.) I would have you stand so I could challenge you to use your gift of party to advance God's kingdom. I would read to you about biblical characters such as Levi:

> Then Levi held a *great banquet* for Jesus at his house, and a *large crowd* of tax collectors and others were eating with them. But the Pharisees and the teachers of the law who belonged to their sect complained to his disciples, "Why do you eat and drink with tax collectors and 'sinners'?" (Luke 5:29-30, emphasis mine).

> *We need to understand and recognize the gift of party.*

It is clear that Levi had the gift of party. The Pharisees seemed to think Jesus partied too much. Would that the world thought the same of us.

I am not talking just about fun and games. I am talking about sharing life. I am talking about getting so close to people that you could call them to watch your kids if you needed to take your spouse to the hospital tonight. If we love them, they will come...and stay. Perhaps that is why Paul said in 1 Corinthians 13:1-3:

> If I speak in the tongues of men and of angels, but have not love, I am only a resounding gong or a clanging cymbal. If I have the gift of prophecy and can fathom all mysteries and all knowledge, and if I have a faith that can move mountains, but have not love, I am nothing. If I give all I possess to the poor and surrender my body to the flames, but have not love, I gain nothing.

Love is spelled t-i-m-e. If you don't have time for your group, they won't have time for you. We have a number of people who can teach and teach well. We affirm them. We love them. We need them. But we need more people who can party for God. If we can enlist an ever-expanding army of Christians who will invite outsiders to the party, we can reach this country for God.

Get serious about having fun. It is the quickest way to double your class in two years or less.

NOTES

[1]Colossians 2:7, on which the Navigators 2:7 series is based. I still believe it is a great series. However, there is a fundamental need of new believers that runs even deeper. New Christians, like children, need food and love.

People Love to Turn You Down—Let Them

Recently I had a fascinating conversation with two friends, a married couple. Both husband and wife had something of a colorful past of drinking and partying. Both had grown up in Christian homes but had turned away from God during their high school and college years. Both honestly admitted, "I hated myself." They hated the fact that they got drunk all the time and couldn't stand themselves when they were sober. Now both are exceedingly happy with Christ, with the church, with their walk with God. They are satisfied customers of the faith.

I posed the same question to both of them: "If someone had suggested that Christianity contained the answer to your problem and the road to a better life, how would you have responded?" They answered as I expected: "I wouldn't have listened." "Christianity" did not convey any positive messages to them. Christianity spoke of condemnation, legalism, distance, irrelevance, and hypocrisy. It did not evoke images of joy, fullness, purpose, hope, and peace. And this is tragic, because if they knew then what they know now, they would have been ready customers. They would have exchanged some painful years for some good years.

Then I asked, "How could the church have communicated to you so that you would hear? How could we have gotten through to you?" They didn't have an answer.

Then it hit me. (Actually it took two days of mulling over the question to figure out the answer.) First, God did the hard part. He began working in their lives, drawing them to himself. He brought them to our church. In addition, you could say that they did their part—they came looking for answers. Yet that did not complete the process of making them disciples. God had done his part; they had done their part. But we needed to do ours.

How did we convince these beer-drinking, fun-loving people that Christ could help them get out of bed in the morning and not hate themselves? Why, unlike many others, did they finally leave their old lifestyle? I thought about the years when they first began to come around. What was it that got them involved and on the path toward living the disciple's life?

Then I remembered the common element: Both had turned me down half a dozen times before they responded positively. Both took about six months to cultivate relationships and assimilate into the group. In short, I had to be willing to be told "no" six times. That was the price that had to be paid.

> *I remembered the common element: Both had turned me down half a dozen times before they responded positively.*

What I didn't know was what had happened each time I called. After we hung up, my friend would say to his wife, "Honey, we need to go to one of these deals one of these times. We really need to get involved." They understood instinctively that they were not getting the full dose of the gospel without being involved in a small group. They hungered to be involved, but they were still hesitant. I simply needed to keep serving them by not giving up. This is just how God treats us, isn't it? He never gives up on us, so we shouldn't give up on others.

It's like the drilling crew that has drilled a half dozen 150-foot wells, all of them dry. Then a local farmer says, "I know where you can find water, and you'll only have to drill ten feet." "Where?" a doubting driller asks skeptically. "Right where you are," explains the farmer, "only ten feet deeper."

The determination to keep digging when it appears that you've dug a dry well will be the key to your success. How willing are you to be turned down? Which of these two churches are you most like?

Church A: "We try to call on every new family in the community within ten days after they move here. Our callers have been trained to be able to identify the good prospects in one visit. In that first call we try to identify the needs of that family and to match them with the appropriate group or class or organization in our church. If they don't respond to that call, we write them off. If they're interested in the church, they'll respond. If they're not interested, there's nothing we can do by continuing to call on them."

Church B: "Our goal is to have one or two of our members call on every newcomer to this community within ten days after they move here. The primary purpose of that first call or two is to build a relationship between our members and the newcomers. With a few rare exceptions we never even consider whether we should continue calling on the newcomers until after we have completed seven or eight calls at that home. Many of our most active members said no when we first invited them to our church... We interpret those first two or three negative responses as meaning, *not-yes, now.* We can't afford to take a no literally!"[1]

> *If you would double your class in two years or less, you will hear "no," "no," "no" before you hear a single "yes."*

How literally do you take "no"? How willing are you to stay with it? If you would double your class in two years or less, you will hear "no," "no," "no" before you hear a single "yes." Some of our most active members are those who told me "no" a half dozen times before they told me "yes."

Robert Kriegel illustrates the same point with the story of Edward Beauvais and America West Airlines. To get the company going, Beauvais and eight other partners took out second mortgages on their homes and used up the credit lines on all their credit cards. Unfortunately, they were still $18 million short! So Beauvais and his partners decided to make a public offering of stock in the company. It required forty trips to Wall Street. "Every major investment banking firm turned us down," Beauvais explains. But after two years, their efforts finally paid off, and since then America West Airlines has raised $250 million from stocks and debentures. Beauvais' conclusion: "You have to be willing to hear 'no' a thousand times. You have to be tenacious... determined to get it."[2]

Kriegel goes on to point out that this kind of persistence doesn't come from a dogged determination that says, "Grit your teeth, tighten your jaw, and push yourself." Rather, "When you're excited about what you are doing, you don't have to convince yourself to 'stick to it,' you have to convince yourself *not* to. *With passion as a base, perseverance comes naturally.*"[3]

The obvious application for us is to fall so in love with Jesus that we become passionate about making disciples of all people, excited that Jesus will use us to spread the message of the gospel. If Edward Beauvais could be that persistent about making money in the airline industry, we should be able to get passionate about making disciples. It is the best way to live and the only way to die.

When I served as class outreach leader, I used to keep careful track of how many times people told me "no." I had a form on which I would write down each invitation, the date, and the person's response. I had personally invited a particular couple to fellowships about a dozen times. Well, it was beginning to become awkward. I had called so many times that I was beginning to wonder if I was becoming a nuisance. I didn't want to bug them. I could just hear them say, "Oh, gee whiz, it's that Josh from the church again. Will he ever stop?" So I decided to take the direct approach and ask. "Listen, I've called a number of times, and I've noticed that ya'll haven't come to anything yet. That's OK, but I was just wondering if I was bothering you. I mean, if you would like, I can quit calling every month." There was a brief silence and then the reply, "Oh, no, keep calling." In other words, we love to turn you down. Just keep on calling.

The Great Commission is worth hearing "no" for. It's a worthy enough cause to feel some rejection for. And hearing "no" will be necessary if you are going to double your class every two years or less. People love to turn you down. Keep on inviting. Keep on asking. Keep on going. Do "not become weary in doing good" (Galatians 6:9).

NOTES

[1] Both church scenarios are taken from Lyle E. Schaller, *Assimilating New Members* (Nashville, TN: Abingdon, 1978), 64.

[2] Robert J. Kriegel and Louis Patler, *If It Ain't Broke...Break It!* (New York, NY: Warner Books, 1991), 17.

[3] Kriegel and Patler, *If It Ain't Broke...Break It!*, 17.

*E*ncourage the group to ministry.

The bottleneck of the evangelistic and disciple-making process has always been a lack of laborers. Jesus told us it would be so. It is the responsibility of those in ministry to recruit those not yet in ministry. An important part of doubling every two years or less is an effective strategy for encouraging people into ministry.

Encouraging the Group to Ministry

Making disciples through small groups is not just about getting people to attend. Nor is it simply about making them active. We often talk about how active people are in church as though that were the goal. But the goal is to make disciples, not to make people active. That is why we must teach halfway decent lessons every week—so we can make disciples. But even teaching a halfway decent lesson is not merely about imparting content; it is about making disciples, about getting people involved in the work of the ministry according to their spiritual gifts.

Jesus told us that we are to be salt and light in a culture that desperately needs him (Matthew 5:13-16). Jesus told us we are to storm the gates of hell and make planet Earth a better place. When Paul came to Ephesus and the Spirit of God worked through him, the church became what it was really supposed to be. As a result, the idol business suffered. It suffered so much that the idol makers organized a rally to stop Paul and the expansion of the church. Can you imagine the church today causing this kind of disturbance? (See Acts 19:23-41.)

Wouldn't you like to be a part of a church that so influenced society that the pornography business was hurt and drug dealers complained of decreased sales? I would. What's more, I think God would be pleased with that. I believe that's why he left us here—not just to evangelize and grow churches and create good people, but to take a society and a culture for God.

When light enters a room, it fills the whole room. Not one part of the room is as it was before. In the same way, when Christians enter a culture and live out the role of being light to the entire world, the world is changed. No part of the world is as it was.

Our role as teachers is not simply to increase attendance. It is not merely to create ethical people. Our role is to be used by God to "turn the world upside down." But in order to do this, we need to get everyone involved in ministry.

> *When light enters a room, it fills the whole room. Not one part of the room is as it was before.*

The bottleneck

So why isn't the church more effective in changing the world? What keeps churches from growing? We have great news. We have a great God. We have a completely sufficient Bible. We have the power of the Holy Spirit. What is the bottleneck? Why are we not more effective than we are in taking our culture for God?

The bottleneck is with the laborers. The problem is the same in every church I visit: a lack of workers. Churches need more preschool workers; they need more youth workers. They need people to serve in the music ministry, people to help with committees. Everywhere you go, from Atlanta to Portland, Houston to New York, Peoria to Manila, the need is the same: We need more workers.

This shouldn't surprise us. Jesus warned us that the bottleneck of the evangelistic and disciple-making process would be with the workers: "He told them, 'The harvest is plentiful, but the workers are few. Ask the Lord of the harvest, therefore, to send out workers into his harvest field'" (Luke 10:2). The problem has always been the shortage of laborers.

That is why we are not seeking merely to get people active or to help people live ethical lives. We are here to get people into the work. It's the only way to get the work done. To get more work done, we need more workers in the work.

What are we going to do about it?

> *I don't know of a church anywhere that could not stand to spend more time asking God to send more workers into the harvest field.*

In addition to warning us that the bottleneck of the process would be the availability of laborers, Jesus taught us what to do about it. He instructed us to pray, to ask God to send workers into the harvest field. We ought to take this command seriously. I don't know of a church anywhere that could not stand to spend more time asking God to send more workers into the harvest field. When we meet for staff meetings, we need to ask the Lord of the harvest to send workers. When we pray at committee meetings, we need to ask God to raise up workers. When we pray in worship, we need to obey the command to pray for helpers. When we pray privately, we need to pray for laborers.

However, we also need to "put feet to our prayers." Nehemiah did this when he prayed to God for protection and then posted a guard to stand watch (Nehemiah 4:9). There is a time to pray and wait on God, and there is a time to pray and act. Jesus' actions in Luke 10 demonstrate that this is a time to pray and act. Jesus didn't stop with an exhortation to pray for workers. He prayed and then sent his disciples out: "Go! I am sending you out like lambs among wolves" (Luke 10:3). In so doing, Jesus modeled the divine recruitment process:

- pray
- send people out

Like Jesus, we need to say to God, "Send workers into the harvest field." Then we need to tell people, "Go!"

Most people need to be encouraged to go into the harvest field. Perhaps they lack confidence. They don't believe that they can make a difference. Perhaps they don't see the urgency. They don't realize the importance of the work. Perhaps they would rather let others do it. For whatever reason, most people need to be nudged into ministry. They need to be told, as Jesus told his disciples, "Go!" It is the responsibility of those of us who are in ministry to recruit those who are not yet in ministry. The onus is on us, not them.

> *It is the responsibility of those who are in ministry to recruit those who are not yet in ministry.*

To draw an analogy from evangelism, is it our responsibility to share the gospel or the responsibility of the lost to find it out? It's our responsibility to tell, don't you think? In a similar way, the onus is on those who are in ministry to recruit those who are not yet in ministry. Jesus told us to pray for workers. Jesus also instructed us to enlist others to the work.

If you want to double your class every two years or less, take seriously the need to pray for and send workers into the harvest field. Take seriously the task of encouraging people toward ministry.

Recruit to a Dream, Not to a Job

If it is the responsibility of those of us in ministry to recruit those who are not yet in ministry, how do we do it?

Jesus challenged his disciples: "Go! I am sending you out like lambs among wolves" (Luke 10:3). Jesus' words remind me in many ways of Winston Churchill's words to the English people during the early years of World War II: "I have nothing to offer but blood, toil, tears, and sweat."

How different this is from much of our recruiting today. We recruit people by telling them that it's not so awful, that it's not that much trouble, that it won't take all that much time. Jesus told his disciples that he was sending them out like lambs among wolves. Translation: You are going to be eaten alive.

What did Jesus know about motivating people that we have missed? Often we operate under the assumption that people are motivated toward that which is pleasant and away from that which is painful. But if this were true, I would think that offering people blood, toil, tears, and sweat would tend to demotivate them. Yet more motivating words have rarely been spoken. Moreover, when Jesus sent the disciples out as sheep among wolves, they actually got out of their chairs and got into the work!

> People are motivated more by a great cause than by comfort.

I conclude that people are motivated more by a great cause than by comfort. We want our lives to count for something. We want to make a difference. If it costs us, so be it. If it is painful, so be it. We want to matter. This is what motivated the disciples to face the wolves. Jesus had called them to be fishers of men. In the words of Dietrich Bonhoeffer, Jesus had bid them to come and die. He had called them to make a difference. Jesus had called them to a vision...and we must do the same.

The starting point in recruiting people is to recruit them to a dream, not merely to a job. Don't recruit people on the basis that a job is not all that much trouble. If you do, what you will get is not all that much. You get what you ask for. So ask people to lay down their lives for something significant. Challenge them to give up their time and their convenience for the noble cause of reaching people with the gospel. Of course, you'll need to recruit people to a dream they really can embrace. Some people respond better to great causes, others to greatness in small chunks. But however you go about it, ask people to go to the mat for something they believe in.

We have the medicine for humanity's sickness. At the core of all of society's problems is sin. The human soul has a disease, and we have the cure. Contrast the pain in the world with the glory of the Kingdom. Read newspaper articles about how life without God actually is. Then challenge the group with the truth that this is not God's plan and that things can be better. We have the solution to the crime problem, the homelessness problem, the drug problem. We have God's solution. The world is acting as expected, but we need to step up to the plate and make a difference on planet Earth.

> *The world is acting as expected, but we need to step up to the plate and make a difference on planet Earth.*

The best recruiting is done individually. It's done face-to-face, phone-to-phone, and heart-to-heart. Recruiting is not relegated to a mass announcement from the pulpit: "We need someone somewhere to help with something over there." This almost never works. What works is getting in someone's face and asking, "What are you doing to serve God and his kingdom? Are you offering yourself to God as a living sacrifice? Do you know the thrill of spiritual battle?" This is the way Jesus recruited: person-to-person, one-on-one.

The best recruiting starts with people and moves them toward ministry, not the other way around. We often start with the vacancy on the organizational chart and try to find someone to fill it. Jesus used a different approach. He started with the person and said, "Go!" Because we care about people and believe that there is no joy like that of spiritual battle, we invite everyone into the game. We start with individuals and move each of them toward ministry.

> *The best recruiting starts with people and moves them toward ministry, not the other way around.*

The best recruiting takes spiritual gifts into consideration. It recognizes that each individual is wired differently and allows each person to express that uniqueness in ministry. Effective recruiting recognizes, in addition to spiritual gifts, a person's temperament, background, and passion. Rick Warren, pastor of Saddleback Valley Community Church, uses a five-part acrostic to help place people in ministry:

S piritual gifts
H eart
A bilities
P ersonality
E xperiences[1]

Rick and the church place people into ministry according to how God has SHAPE'd them. We ought to do the same. At the very least, we need to teach regularly on the spiritual gifts. Anyone who sits in your class for two years or more ought to be able to identify his or her spiritual gift without hesitating.

The best recruiting gives people specific options. Suppose you were purchasing a Christmas present. Which would be more helpful to you: a blank order form on which you can write whatever you want, or a colorful catalog that gives you a list of choices? Most people respond best when they're given a specific list of choices.

In the next chapter, we'll explore seven small-group ministry options: teacher, inreach leader, outreach leader, fellowship leader, hospitality leader, prayer leader, and class president. Most people are able to match their gifts to one or two of these choices. If they can, I challenge them to use their gifts to help grow the group. I have been guilty, on occasion, of telling people, "Discover your spiritual gifts, and then go do something helpful. Find something, anything to do." But people respond better when we show them a list of seven roles and ask, "Do any of these make sense to you? Would you like to experiment with one of these for a semester?"

The best recruiting allows for the creative, entrepreneurial spirit. Most people will choose one of the seven options, but some will want to create their own ministries. Someone will want to start a food closet for the homeless. Another will want to form a volleyball league to assimilate outsiders into the body. Yet another will volunteer for the music ministry. We need to let people follow their God-given creativity.

The best recruiting allows people time to get well. We must recognize that not everyone is ready for ministry. Some people need to come to the hospital as patients, not as doctors or nurses. Some people have been beaten up by the world and need time to recover. They don't need the pressure of someone begging them to help. I have had broken and hurting friends who, when they finally found their way back to church, were told, "Around here, everyone is expected to be a minister. We don't need anyone sitting on the bench. We have enough deadwood. If you're not going to get with it, get lost." That is not a very kind thing to say to people who need to get well. After Jesus had healed Peter's mother-in-law from her fever, "She got up at once and began to wait on them" (Luke 4:39). That's how people are. Once they get well, they will naturally want to help. But not before.

The best recruiting allows people to say "no." There is a fine line between recruitment and manipulation, between challenging people and controlling people, between inspiring people and making them feel guilty.

> *Love always leaves people with a choice.*

We must always remember that the gospel is all about grace. Guilt is not the good news. This fine line has to do with recognizing the boundary between you and me. I can only invite; you can accept or decline. If you aren't free to accept or to decline, it's not an invitation. If you aren't free to turn me down, it is slavery, not Christianity. We can invite and encourage people to ministry, but we must leave them with a choice. Love always leaves people with a choice.

The best recruiting honors people's time. We have a slogan at my church: one person, one job. In case you hadn't noticed, people are busy these days. What's worse, some people who volunteered their time in the past have been taken advantage of. They volunteered to do a little, and the leadership demanded more. The

> *We have a slogan at my church: one person, one job.*

leaders wouldn't honor their "no," so now they are reluctant to do anything at all. It is far better to get ten people working than to have one person do the work of ten people.

The best recruiting utilizes all the time that people have. At times people can handle the work of ten. Let them. Maybe someone retired early with a full salary and benefits and has years of health and vitality to use for God. We need to involve that person in the work. We need to show people in situations like this how they can spend their lives advancing God's kingdom instead of hitting a little white ball around a golf course. We need to offer these people part-time jobs at the church, pay them a dollar a year, designate them associate pastors, and put their names on the church stationery. We need to allow them to visit the hospital, take care of administrative matters, start a new ministry, or do whatever they have the gifts and the passion to do. People will do for God what they would never do for money. But sometimes we get limited time because we ask for limited time. There are times to ask people for their lives. Jesus did.

The best recruiting cares for the worker and for the work. As in many areas of life, balance is everything. We need to care about people. We need to allow them time to get well and permit them to turn us down. But we should also care about the work. We should care enough to follow Jesus' example of valuing the worker and the work. In a sense, this is what the fight between Paul and Barnabas was all about (Acts 15:36-40). Paul argued that the work was too important to entrust to John Mark, a quitter. Barnabas, however, believed that John Mark mattered to God, that there was grace, and that John Mark needed someone to believe in him. Paul argued for the importance of the work, Barnabas for the importance of the worker. Both were half right.

> *Catch someone doing something right and brag to high heaven about it.*

The best recruiting shows people how. No one wants to try and fail. If you ask people to help, be prepared to show them exactly what is needed and how they can successfully meet that need. Moreover, be ready to give continual feedback—especially positive feedback—all along the way. Catch someone doing something right and brag to high heaven about it. People need far more carrots than sticks. So dole out corrections in small dosages.

Here is a simple training process that incorporates all these principles: (1) Let them watch you. (2) Work together. (3) Watch them. (4) Let them work on their own.

Suppose you were recruiting a couple to be your hospitality leaders. You want them to give Friday nights to Jesus every other Friday night. Here's how you could use this process to train them:

● **Let them watch you.** Invite them to your home for an informal evening of cards and Diet Coke. Involve a new visitor. Let the couple see the potential. Help them see that this is something they could do.

● **Work together.** Invite another couple over to their home. You might also want them to watch you call and make the invitation. Explain that you normally invite a couple early in the week and confirm on Thursday and that you invite no more than one or two new couples at a time. Explain the benefits of including another couple from the group as well.

- **Watch them.** Have them invite a couple over. You come over again, but this time you take a more passive role. Let them lead the evening. Let them be in charge. You're there for moral support. When the evening is over, tell them how great they will do at this and how much you believe in them. Tell them they will make a difference. Look them in the eye and tell them that planet Earth is going to be more habitable because of their ministry.

- **Let them work on their own.** Ultimately, this is the goal of ministry—people functioning on their own. We help them use their gifts to grow their group. We challenge them to take ownership of the ministry, but people still need to be encouraged. We will forever and always need to tell people, "Well done." A big part of our role is to encourage people in ministry.

This four-step process is considerably more work than simply telling people that giving Friday nights to Jesus is a good idea and that they should think about doing it. It's also about a million times more effective. In most cases, it is the difference between success and failure. One reason we don't have more people in the ministry is because we don't use an effective process for ensuring their success in ministry.

The best recruiting pays as much attention to people already working as it does to the new recruit. It takes far more energy to recruit someone to start in ministry than to encourage someone to stay in ministry. It takes only a little energy to keep people going, but it does take some. So we need to constantly say thank you to the people on our team.

Finally, the best recruiting recruits to a team. There is far too much thought of individual effort in ministry. Ministry at its best is done in teams. In fact, teamwork in ministry is so crucial that it's the subject of the next chapter.

> *It takes far more energy to recruit someone to start in ministry than to encourage someone to stay in ministry.*

NOTES

[1] Rick Warren, *The Purpose Driven Church* (Grand Rapids, MI: Zondervan, 1995), 370.

Teamwork 24

Many people think in terms of fulfilling the Great Commission one person at a time. That is, I share the gospel with someone, who grows and shares the gospel with someone else, and so on. This book takes a different approach.

I remember once telling a group, "I can hardly wait until I win a person to Christ, disciple him, and then see him win someone else to Christ. I'd like to be a spiritual grandparent." I thought this was a noble goal. One of the group members, however, didn't. He rebuffed me: "If you could do that, you wouldn't need the body." In hindsight, I think he was right.

This book is not about reaching one, who reaches one, who reaches one. This is about working together in groups so the entire group reproduces every two years or less. This is about teamwork, not solo performance.

I believe God thinks in terms of teams. That is what the body of Christ is all about—working together to advance the Kingdom. The hand accomplishes very little alone. In the same way, no individual believer has all the necessary gifts to do what needs to get done. But working together, we can accomplish more than we every dreamed possible.

Has it ever struck you as strange that, when Jesus sent out the disciples, he felt it important to cut the number of possible "teams" in half by sending them out in teams of two? Jesus could have had twelve individuals out preaching, but he thought it was better to have six teams than twelve individuals. Jesus knew the value of a team.

There are at least seven reasons you need a team surrounding you, helping you get the work done, working with you to fulfill the Great Commission.

> Where two or three are gathered together, there is synergy.

Teams create synergy. Where two or three are gathered together, there is synergy. The total is greater than the sum of the parts because, in this case, $1 + 1 + 1 = 4$. Three people working together accomplish four times as much as they would if each were working independently. Together, the coals keep the fire hot. Thus, a teacher working with an outreach leader and an inreach leader can accomplish far more than any one of them could alone.

We all have limited time. Synergy isn't the only reason to have a team. There is also a limited number of hours in a week—168, to be exact. No one has ever created even one hour more. These 168 hours must include sleeping, eating, working, spending time with the family, showering, dressing, quiet time, resting, waiting, preparing your lesson, time in church, chores around the house, and so on, and so on, and so on. The point is, you don't have a lot of time left to devote to your class and to the things that will help you double your class in two years, even if you want to. The time simply isn't available—not unless you mortgage your family, cheat your employer, or skimp on your quiet time.

No one has ever been able to break the 168-hours-per-week limit. Prophets and kings, beggars and sages—all live under the same limit. So if we want to accomplish a great deal, we can only do so by including others on our team. We cannot do it all, but everyone can do a little. With a team working together, all the limited resources we bring together add up to an awful lot.

People want to be used. Do not think that I am advocating using people in the sense of manipulating them. Nothing could be further from the truth. Rather, I have a basic conviction that people want to help. My sons want to help. When they were young, they would have helped most by getting out of the way. But they wanted to help, so I let them. In the same way, there are people in your class who want to help you. They want to be a part of something significant. They want to help double the class in two years or less. If you believe in them enough to put them to work, you'll increase their self-esteem and improve their helping skills. Moreover, they will discover their gifts and will feel assimilated into the group. We develop people, not only by affirming them, but also by believing in them enough to entrust to them what is near and dear to our heart: the work of the ministry.

> *We develop people, not only by affirming them, but also by believing in them enough to entrust to them what is near and dear to our heart: the work of the ministry.*

You get more people thinking. When people are involved, they think about how to do the job better. Do you know what? Some of their ideas are better than yours or mine! The more little think tanks we have, the better our chances of discovering breakthrough methods of reaching the lost and leading them to live the disciple's life. When class members sit passively on the sidelines, they are not thinking on that level. Get

117

them involved, and watch their brains shift into high gear.

It's biblical! According to Exodus 18:13-26, Moses assembled a team to help govern the people. (We'll look at that passage in more detail shortly.) Likewise, Acts 6:1-7 reports that the early church enlisted deacons to help the apostles with the work. In addition, Ephesians 4:11-12 teaches that the role of pastors is to equip people to help with the work, and I have already noted that Christ sent the disciples out in pairs. Needless to say, the Bible is big on groups and teams. It is solidly behind fellowship, community, unity, and togetherness.

The work is too big for one person. I love the view of a city at night—all those lights glistening like a string of Christmas lights in a pile on the floor. When I fly into a city at night, I often think, "So many people." We are debtors to those people—debtors who have been loved and who must love, debtors obligated to communicate the gospel to them in language they understand, debtors to show them how to live the disciple's life.[1] There is only one way to get a large job done, and that is to get a large number of people working on it. We can run a typical church program with a handful of people, but we need an army to transform culture. We have an army, but we need to get everyone involved in the work.

> *Q: How do you swallow an elephant? A: One bite at a time.*

Q: How do you swallow an elephant? A: One bite at a time. The pastor can't do it all alone. The staff can't do it all alone. You as a teacher can't do it all alone. But if each of you surrounds yourself with three to five people who can work together, you have some hope of getting the work done.

By the way, I am not talking about asking people to do your work. I'm encouraging you to give them a slice of the work that God gave to all of us. There is a world of difference.

Teams are fun. What we say about marriage—"When there is joy, it is doubled; when there is sorrow, it is halved"—is also true of groups. It's fun to work alongside a team of people, each one using his or her gifts to grow the group. It's fun to work with a team to get the job done. So now let's look at some options in putting together a team.

The players on the team

I invite you to consider three ways of organizing your team. You may think of other ways or of some combination of these three; the important thing is to create a team that works in your setting.

1. In a very small class, you can do it all.

If your class has fewer than six members, you don't need to worry about a team. You can do all the contacting, organizing, and arranging that needs to be done. This is often how new classes begin. The nice thing about doing it yourself is that you know that everything is getting done. But if you do your job well, it will soon grow, and you will need to give part of it away. This is, after all, the point: to grow classes by teaching people and then giving them a piece of the action.

2. A seven-member team

As the group grows, you may want to develop a seven-member team. This is the most sensible arrangement for a midsize class (ten to twenty members). These are the team members:

- teacher
- inreach leader
- outreach leader
- fellowship leader
- hospitality leader
- prayer leader
- class president

The **teacher** is responsible to present a halfway decent lesson each and every week—nothing less will do. Enough said.

The **inreach leader** takes care of everyone whose name appears on the class roster. This person loves class members, keeps up with their lives, invites them to every fellowship every month, and helps shepherd them toward spiritual maturity. I suggest that the inreach leader also take roll and contact people who are absent.

> *The inreach leader takes care of everyone whose name appears on the class roster.*

The inreach leader should make sure that every member who is absent receives a card. I suggest writing cards to absentees right there in class. At our church, we furnish the cards, pay the postage, and have groups leave the cards in a designated place for mailing on Monday. Once I worked with a group that circulated a sheet titled "We missed you." The inreach leader wrote each absentee's name on a sheet and then passed the sheets around. The entire group had an opportunity to write personal notes to the people who were absent. This proved to be very effective. Writing cards in class is quick and easy, and it assures you that it will get done.

The **outreach leader** is responsible for everyone whose name is not on the class roster. Sometimes there's confusion: Someone has attended three times—is she the inreach leader's responsibility or the outreach leader's responsibility? Answer: If her name appears on the class roll, she is the inreach leader's responsibility; if not, she is the outreach leader's.

> *The outreach leader is responsible for everyone whose name is not on the class roster.*

Give your outreach leader the freedom to discover creative ways to involve people in outreach and to assimilate new people into the life of the group. But don't forget the two most effective ways: (1) inviting every prospect to every fellowship every month and (2) giving Friday nights to Jesus. Encourage your outreach leader to be friendly, real, and personal with the outsiders.

You as a teacher should remain personally active in outreach. Just as a pastor has a unique role in leading the church in outreach, so the teacher has a unique role in attracting new members. You can delegate, but stay involved. Open your own home from time to time. Do some of the inviting yourself.

The **fellowship leader** plans fellowships as often as the group wants them. If you've never planned a fellowship, you probably don't have an adequate appreciation for how much work it is. Someone has to set up the baby-sitting, buy the streamers, arrange the meeting place, and so forth. As I said earlier, all good ideas degenerate into work. Although the fellowship leader may not plan the details of every fellowship, this person is responsible for making everything happen. One way to lighten the load is to assign a different person to help plan the fellowship every month.

The **hospitality leader** gives Friday nights to Jesus. This person invites over some friends, some absentees, and some new people to have a lot of fun together. It is an important part of the work. If the teacher is doing a halfway decent job with teaching, this person can single-handedly double the group.

The **prayer leader** prays for the group *and* encourages the group to pray. If the church already has an organized prayer ministry, the prayer leader can encourage people to get on board. Some, however, will want to organize prayer chains or coordinate prayer breakfasts from time to time.

You should encourage the prayer leader to do whatever works. I know one prayer leader who called every class member every week and asked for prayer requests. The last I heard, that class was growing rapidly.

The **class president** sees that it all gets done. After I figured out the six previous roles, I began challenging teachers to recruit their teams. I generally got blank stares. Teachers love to teach, but they're often bored with parties and organization. They need help with these details. The class president helps the teacher get everyone working. Class presidents tend to be well-organized and good at delegating. They have the gift of pointing people in the right direction: "Bob, you take care of this. Sue, you get onto that." Once someone in a conference asked me, "How do you get teachers to do outreach?" My answer: "I don't. I let the class president recruit, train, and direct people who are gifted in outreach, and then I let them do the work."

Effective teachers will find people to do what the teachers have very little interest in doing—seeing that every member and every prospect is invited to a fellowship every month, for example. Then they can concentrate on sitting at home reading dusty commentaries.

If you don't have strong administrative or leadership skills; if you do not like maintaining a system, motivating people, and keeping up with details; if your first and only love is teaching the Bible and not managing people; if you are bored silly by some of the methods in this book, I have good news for you.

There is a place for you in the kingdom of God! God *does* have a place for people who love to pore over dusty commentaries but who are not sure they can invite every member and every visitor to every fellowship every month. However, you will never be as effective as God wants until you surround yourself with a team of people with complementary gifts.

You may want to pray all night for wisdom in selecting the key player who can make it all happen—the class president. This person's job description is pretty broad: See that everything (except teaching) that needs to be done gets done. Class presidents are the kind of people who have fat, three-ring binders and complicated to-do lists. They like pro formas, job descriptions, and flow charts. These people can be used greatly by God to get the rest of the body operating and functioning as it should.

This makes life much simpler for you, the teacher. You can worry about presenting a great lesson while the class president worries about the rest. You're responsible for presenting a halfway decent lesson every week. The class president is responsible for doing everything necessary to see that the group doubles every two years or less. This generally works out well in terms of spiritual gifts, because most people who love to study and teach don't like to mess with anything else. We need to turn the teaching over to the teachers and the doing over to the doers.

> *The goal is obedience to the Great Commission, not symmetry in organization.*

This seven-person team can work in various configurations. In many cases, one person will fill several roles. Perhaps one person can oversee outreach *and* fellowship. These are two big jobs, but some people are up to the challenge. Above all else, be creative and flexible. Use the people God gives you and the gifts God has given them to do what God has told us all to do. The goal is obedience to the Great Commission, not symmetry in organization.

3. Leaders of ten (LOTs)

When Jethro visited Moses, his son-in-law, he gave him some enduring advice on managing large groups (Exodus 18:14-25). The Jethro plan was to arrange a large number of people into a pyramid structure so that no leader cared for more than about ten people. I have organized groups in a similar way, recruiting a team of people who would care for ten people each. In a small group, this combines the roles of inreach leader and outreach leader. You simply assign ten people—some members, some prospects—to leaders in your group. Each leader serves as pastor to the ten. If you have a large group, you can appoint a second layer of leaders, each responsible for ten small-group leaders. That was Jethro's plan for taking care of the people of Israel.

My study of Exodus 18:14-25 also revealed a number of other principles that apply to organizing a large group. Just for fun, why don't you read Exodus 18:14-25 and see if you agree with the ones I discuss on the next few pages?

> *Don't confuse activity with results.*

Working harder is not necessarily working smarter. Moses would have received a gold medal if awards were based on hard work. But the rewards don't go to the one who sweats the most; they go to the one who gets the most done. Sunup until sundown—working hard was not Moses' problem. In the same way, many of us become addicted to work because it feeds our desire to feel needed. Perhaps this was true of Moses. He may have been tired, but at least he knew he was needed, important. But he wasn't effective. There were long lines of people with unmet needs at the end of every day. We need to be effective, not busy. We need to get the job done. So don't confuse activity with results.

Ten is a good span of responsibility. The highest level of care and responsibility in Jethro's plan was one to ten. It's pretty tough to do much more. People can care for ten; they cannot care for fifty. Even the leaders of fifty, one hundred, and so on seem to have been set up in a pyramid structure so that no one was directly

> *We may get more done if we give people less to do.*

responsible for more than ten people. The lesson is clear. We may get more done if we give people less to do.

The leader's job is to recruit and train other leaders. Moses selected and taught the leaders, but he didn't choose just anyone. He selected people who met high spiritual qualifications: "capable men from all the people—men who fear God, trustworthy men who hate dishonest gain" (Exodus 18:21). Moses was also responsible to teach the leaders he selected how to succeed. Jethro told him to "teach them the decrees and laws, and show them the way to live and the duties they are to perform" (Exodus 18:20). This is our job as well: to recruit qualified individuals and teach them how to succeed. We are also to do one other thing.

The other job of the leader is to represent the people before God. Jethro told Moses, "You must be the people's representative before God" (Exodus 18:19b). At the very least, this involves prayer. The leader has an ongoing responsibility to pray for the people. This truth was also recognized by the apostles during the early days of the church: "[We] will give our attention to prayer and the ministry of the word" (Acts 6:4). Prayer, teaching, and recruiting people to the work are three responsibilities of all leaders.

Need does not necessarily indicate God's will for our lives. Moses' explanation of why he was working so hard can be summarized in one word: need. The job needed to be done. Unfortunately, Moses was under the illusion that, because there was a need, he was to meet it. We can be tempted to think the same thing: Because there are needs, we are obligated

> *Sometimes the only way others will pick up the ball is if we drop it.*

to meet those needs. Mature leaders, however, can look need in the face and say, "No. Not me. Not today." Wise leaders know they cannot do everything. They are in touch with their humanity. They also care enough about the work to involve other people in it. Sometimes the only way others will pick up the ball is if we drop it.

Burning the candle at both ends is a sure way to burn out. Jethro warned Moses that, if things kept going the way they were, both Moses and the people would burn out. It was exhausting on both ends, tiring for Moses and for the people standing in line. According to Jethro, the situation wasn't good: "What you are doing is not good. You and these people who come to you will only wear yourselves out. The work is too heavy for you; you cannot handle it alone" (Exodus 18:17b-18).

> *Christian ministry ought to become lighter and lighter as we learn to do it better and better.*

Delegation will lighten your load. Many Christians are addicted to work. Somehow we have swallowed the lie that the busier we are the more important we are. Moses was important, but not because he was busy. In fact, following God's plan for his life actually made his load lighter (Exodus 18:22). In a similar way, Jesus said, "My yoke is easy and my burden is light" (Matthew 11:30). If ministry isn't easy for you, look to see whose yoke you are carrying. Christian ministry ought to become lighter and lighter as we learn to do it better and better. So if the work of the ministry isn't becoming easier for you, reevaluate what you're doing.

Jethro taught Moses that, as he followed God's plan, it would be good for Moses as well as for the people (Exodus 18:23). Delegation benefits everyone—the leader who delegates, the people delegated to, and the people who receive the ministry. Everyone is a winner.

Conclusion

I've been told that the entire McDonald's organization exists to make sure that a sixteen-year-old employee holding down her first job can successfully deliver fresh, hot, crisp French fries across a counter in thirty seconds or less. The entire organization exists to make the person on the front line successful. McDonald's has built one of the largest food-service organizations in the world using teenagers whose parents cannot get them to clean their rooms. Our job is much easier. We simply need to give team leaders—whether they are outreach leaders, inreach leaders, LOTs, or some other ministry leaders—everything they need to be successful in *their* ministries.

Let me invite you to see the big picture. We have a teacher presenting a halfway decent lesson each and every week, challenging people to live the disciple's life. Beside the teacher is someone who is planning a fellowship every month—bowling this month, a picnic next month, and so on. Beside the fellowship leader is someone who is inviting every member of the class to these fellowships. People who might otherwise have become inactive remain part of the group because of these regular contacts. Beside the fellowship leader is an outreach leader inviting class prospects to attend these fellowships. Beside the outreach leader are two hospitality leaders giving every other Friday night to Jesus. They're opening their homes and playing cards and eating coffeecake and sipping Diet Coke and laughing a lot. They invite absentees and prospects whom the inreach leader and the outreach leader tell them about. Leading and supporting them is a class president who organizes the whole thing. Most important, we have a prayer leader who is bathing the whole process is prayer.

This group can easily double every two years or less. It can double without doing violence to who God has made the members to be. The members can do it within the context of each one's spiritual gifts. They can do it without sacrificing time for family life. They can do it, and it can be fun.

With groups functioning together like this, we can take our nation for God. What a glorious sight: each person using his or her gifts to grow his or her group. Advancing the Kingdom together.

NOTES

[1] When Paul declares, "I am *obligated* both to Greeks and non-Greeks, both to the wise and the foolish" (Romans 1:14), he uses a Greek word that implies "indebtedness." In short, Paul was a "debtor" to those who had not yet heard.

"Election" Day

A recent Gallup survey indicated that, on average, 10 percent of a church's members are involved in ministry. Another 50 percent say they have no interest whatsoever in ministry. The astonishing discovery is that 40 percent say they would be happy to be involved in ministry. They simply haven't been asked to help or don't know how.[1] We need to get them involved. We need to ask them to help and show them how.

One practical way to get people involved is to give them the ministry choices outlined in Chapter 24 and then "elect" them to those positions. Many classes follow a quarterly literature cycle, and this can serve as a reminder to hold an election day. Another approach might be to hold an election day at the beginning of the winter, spring, summer, and fall semesters. However, feel free to hold an election as often as you need. On this day, you can "elect" people—they may actually be volunteering—to fill some of the positions discussed in Chapter 24: class president, inreach leader, outreach leader, fellowship leader, hospitality leader, and prayer leader.

Because of the depth of knowledge that is helpful to the task of teaching, I do not recommend that you elect a new teacher each time. Keeping the same teacher also serves to give some continuity to the group. However, vary the organization to meet your specific needs. I know of groups with more than one teacher. I've also seen groups with two class presidents and others without any class president. This variety is OK. It's part of owning the ministry.

The growth of a movement is directly related to the depth and breadth of the involvement of its people.

Instead of electing only one person to each position, you may want to ask everyone to sign up for one of the roles. Several of the roles can easily have several people working on them, especially in larger classes. To make sure no one is left out, the class president can assume responsibility for asking everyone who is not there on election day, "Where would you like to serve? Would you like to help with inreach, outreach, hospitality, or prayer? Perhaps you'd like to help teach." People can, of course, bow out, but expecting them to bow in communicates the idea that every member is a minister. We often say we believe that, but our expectation generally isn't there. By asking everyone to serve in a role that corresponds to his or her giftedness, we put feet to the idea that we want all hands on deck. Remember: The growth of a movement is directly related to the depth and breadth of the involvement of its people.

There are several advantages to holding an election day once a quarter.

Regular election days remind people of the importance of the task and of their involvement in it. Holding an election allows you the opportunity to redream the dream. You can and should talk about the vision of taking your community for Christ through groups that are doubling every two years or less. You can talk about thoroughly assimilating one new couple or two new people every three months. You can describe what it means for every member to be a minister. You can remind class members that people who are opposed to the gospel are not opposed to ice cream. Retell the stories of people in the class and how they came into the group. Let people talk about their first impressions of the class and what it has meant to them since.

People are more likely to sign up for something for a specific (and short) period of time. People don't want to sign up for something for life, especially if they've never done anything like it before. They may serve the rest of their lives, but it's nice to know the train has some getting-off places along the way. So ask people if they would be willing to experiment with something for a semester. Trial and error is one of the best ways of discovering spiritual gifts. We don't discover giftedness by reading books as much as by doing ministry.

> *We don't discover giftedness by reading books as much as by doing ministry.*

It allows people who are ineffective in one area of ministry to gracefully move to another. When people aren't succeeding, you don't have to fire them—you can simply reassign them. No one is good at everything, but everyone is good at something. Reevaluating every quarter allows for a gracious escape when something isn't working. If you've ever faced the difficulty of dealing with people who've had a ministry role for which they were not suited, you understand the genius of this plan. It is hard to fire people. It is far easier to ask, "Why don't you try this for a quarter?"

> *No one is good at everything, but everyone is good at something.*

It allows you to keep and affirm people who have found their areas of giftedness. If people want, they can serve in the same positions quarter after quarter, year after year. There are no term limits. The quarterly election is simply an affirmation that they're doing a good job and a reminder to keep up the good work. You can't brag about people too much: "Bob and Mary are doing such a great job of hospitality—what do you say we ask them to do it for their sixty-third quarter?"

It allows people to serve in various roles over time. Several spiritual gifts enable a person to serve in a variety of roles. The gift of service, for example, may equip someone to serve as fellowship leader, inreach leader, or outreach leader. There is something to be said for giving people some variety in service. Even if they're gifted at something and love it, they may want to do something else for a while. Variety is the spice of life.

It allows people to take a break, knowing that they can get back in later. People love to serve, and most will do so year after year if we don't burn them out along the way. When we allow people to graciously take a quarter off and then return to ministry, they're renewed and invigorated, ready to get back to the task. But there is nothing more exhausting than serving when you can't take a break.

It allows the body to affirm people's giftedness. Sometimes people don't know whether they're gifted at something or not. But it means everything when the group says, "You should try this position. I think you would do really well at it." I didn't know I had a gift for teaching until several people approached me after I had taught and said, "You're really good at teaching; I really learned a lot." Election day once a quarter allows everyone to experience affirmations like this.

Allow plenty of latitude in the way you conduct an election. It may be a matter of asking people to volunteer. It may be a matter of a strong-handed leader lovingly but firmly assigning positions. Or you may want to hold an honest-to-goodness election. The means will vary according to the personality of your group. However you do it, the tradition of a quarterly election day does a lot to keep the group growing and doubling every two years or less.

NOTES

[1] Rick Warren, *The Purpose Driven Church* (Grand Rapids, MI: Zondervan, 1995), 366.

Reproduce new groups.

Reproducing a group has always been difficult on any level. But reproduction is the key to the survival of future generations. There is no other way. Doubling your class does not mean going from ten members to twenty. That is easy. Doubling means going from one group to two.

What If It Works?

What if it works? What if you invite every member and every prospect to every fellowship every month? What if you give Friday nights to Jesus and end up doubling your class in two years or less? If it works, you'll be faced with one of the biggest problems known to adult education in churches: how to divide the class. (Because it is so offensive, we usually don't even use the word "divide." Rather, we speak of "creating new units" or something similar.) I've known many ministers of education who have sacrificed their careers by trying to force classes to divide. I've also seen situations in which classes grew to forty, divided, and then turned into two classes of ten. Just recently I heard of a new minister of education coming to a large church and dividing many of the adult classes. The result? Mass exodus. It seems that many people would rather not be at that church at all than not be in the group of their choice. It remains to be seen how long it will be before the minister of education joins the exodus.

> *We are in the small-group business, and growth will put us out of business. If we grow, we'll cease to be a small group.*

Not this minister of education. I don't force mandatory class splits. Yet the importance of dividing classes is obvious. We are in the small-group business, and growth will put us out of business. If we grow, we'll cease to be a small group. We'll become a big group, then a small congregation, and finally a big congregation. Now there is nothing wrong with big congregations, but we need small groups, too. We need a means of effectively and peacefully reproducing small groups.

Let me candidly admit that there are no easy options here. However you do it, it will involve saying goodbye to old friends so you can befriend people who are not yet friends with Jesus. This is inherently difficult. But I do have some ideas that will make it a little easier.

One way to create new units is to subdivide the class without telling anyone what you're doing. Do not under any circumstances tell people you are dividing the class. Explain to them that you are subdividing into prayer circles, discussion circles, care groups, or something innocuous like that.

This has worked effectively for me on three occasions. Once a group of young married adults grew to nearly twenty-five in average attendance. Discussion was suffering. People were slipping through the cracks. Our appeal—being a warm, close, loving fellowship—was killing us by destroying the warm, close, loving fellowship. I could have told the group, "OK, we are going to divide. Everyone over age twenty-seven, go to this room; everyone twenty-seven or under, go to that room." But this inevitably produces disastrous results.

So we decided to have the best of both worlds, to be together and separate at the same time. We originally tried staying together for part of the hour and breaking up into small groups for the rest of the hour. To maintain continuity, I prepared questions for the discussion leaders to use within the small groups. As time went on, however, people requested more time for the smaller groups. So I began to write the entire lesson for the small groups and then went off and taught another class.[1] It's a little like getting kids to eat something by having them try a bite or two. When people feel the warmth of a small group, it will meet a need in their lives that the large-group experience cannot touch. Large groups are by nature content-oriented, whereas small groups are relationship-oriented. In a group of thirty, few people will talk on a regular basis, but nearly everyone in a group of eight will talk freely every week. This is how relationships are born.

Another way to give birth to a new group is to ask a strong, "charismatic" leader to launch it. In this case, everything rises and falls on leadership. If you have a capable leader who is willing to do so, that person can single-handedly form a new group. This assumes that people are willing to follow, but that is implied when we label someone a strong leader. (No followers, no leaders.) Occasionally you will discover a leader strong enough to take a handful of people and form a new group without any help. Most leaders, however, are not that strong. They need some help getting going. That is why we have a third method.

The best way to start a new group is for *you* to move to an alternate time or curriculum and to leave those who won't come along with someone else. Because you are the leader, it's almost certain that at least half the group will come along with you. But because people

> *The best way to start a new group is for* you *to move to an alternate time or curriculum and to leave those who won't come along with someone else.*

are creatures of habit, you're almost guaranteed that enough people will stay behind to keep the old class going. This is the most effective way of starting new classes I know.

Every time we start a new congregation, we depend on several established groups to form the core of the new congregation. People follow leaders. A very effective church-growth strategy is to launch multiple congregations meeting in the same building. One example of this is to start a contemporary service on Saturday night or at 9:45 Sunday morning. To do this, the church needs several existing groups to move to the new hour. This is also a very effective way to start new groups. People move in groups; people follow leaders.[2]

Another approach that is a little less radical than starting an entirely new group is for the teacher to change topics of study. If you choose something that's interesting to half the group but not to the rest, you're almost certain to successfully create a new group. An example of this is to have a young-couples class divide so the parents in the group can study parenting for a quarter. If half the group doesn't yet have children, it will divide rather nicely. We've taken a similar approach with psychological issues. Some people like them, while others think of them as psychobabble.

> *A key value here is that people feel that they have a choice and can make whatever choice they desire.*

A key value here is that people feel that they have a choice and can make whatever choice they desire. This is much more effective than saying to people, "You go here; you go there." It is far better to say, "Next quarter, instead of one class we'll have two choices. You can continue doing what you're doing, or you can join Mary Ellen in a study of biblical principles of parenting."

Couples look forward to bearing children. Parents look forward to having grandchildren. They proudly sport pictures in their wallets and purses. Growth is normal—it is a sign of health. Every class should look forward to the day when it can give birth to other groups.

My experience has been that it's sometimes easier for a group to give birth to three or four groups simultaneously than to give birth to one. For one thing, if the group grows large enough, everyone will see that it is not a small group any longer and will thus see the need to create a new group. As a group grows to twenty-five, some will see the need for a new group. But when it reaches forty, everyone will recognize that it is no longer a small group. It may be easier at this point to divide into three or four groups than it would to divide a group of twenty-five into two groups. Waiting until everyone sees the need will go a long way toward smoothing the process of group multiplication. The key will be finding the available teachers needed to lead each group. The bottleneck of the disciple-making process has always been laborers. We must be vigilant in addressing this need.

To do so, teachers need apprentices into whose lives they can pour their own lives. This is the spirit of 2 Timothy 2:2, "And the things you have heard me say in the presence of many witnesses entrust to reliable men who will also be qualified to teach others." Everything rises and falls on leadership. The greatest thing anyone in ministry can achieve is to produce a steady stream of other leaders. Ideally, every inreach leader should be training another inreach leader, every prayer leader another prayer leader, and so forth. It's amazing how much of church growth is simple obedience to what God has told us to do. In short, if we will simply obey 2 Timothy 2:2, we will double our classes.

> *Everything rises and falls on leadership.*

When we talk about doubling a class every two years or less, we are not talking primarily about going from ten people to twenty. Four hundred pieces of mail will do that in one week. We are talking about creating new groups with new leaders. This is the real key to the growth of the movement.

> *When we talk about doubling a class every two years or less, we are not talking primarily about going from ten people to twenty.*

NOTES

[1] These lessons are being posted onto the World Wide Web and can be downloaded or printed from http://www.joshhunt.com.

[2] This concept is detailed in my previous book, *Let It Grow!* (Grand Rapids, MI: Baker Books, 1993).

Groups of Groups

As a church grows, it will quickly become a congregation of congregations, a group of groups. And as we strengthen the life of each group, there is a tendency for loyalty to the whole to decrease. As we start new ministries, new worship services, and new groups, we become increasingly pluralistic. And when this happens, people typically respond in one of two ways.

This first and perhaps most common response is to bemoan this diversity as bad, unspiritual, and unbiblical. Groups with a strong group life and internal loyalty are perceived as being against the church as a whole. The dagger is drawn with the saying, "They are just a church to themselves, a separate church." Lyle Schaller, however, rightly observes:

> Many church leaders tend to focus on the negative values of closely knit, cohesive groups rather than seeing them as foundation stones for the evangelistic outreach of that congregation and in the assimilation of new members. Too often these small groups are seen as cliques, rivals, power blocs, and closed clubs. The ironic part of this is that the more meaningful membership in that small face-to-face group is to the persons in it, the more threatening it often appears to be to the individuals not in it.[1]

Critics of small-group loyalty focus on church unity, love, and fellowship. Indeed, these are points worthy of serious consideration, for the New Testament places a premium on love, unity, and related values. In fact, Jesus taught that love is the central criterion by which his church could be judged (John 13:35). However, it does not necessarily follow that the stronger the small-group life (and, as a result, the weaker the loyalty to all-church activities), the weaker the level of love. In fact, it normally works the other way. A strong emphasis on all-church activities will likely produce fewer close friendships and actually lessen the level of love in the congregation.

Another response to increased diversity is to emphasize *both* a strong group life and all-church activities. There is something to be said for this. First, no matter how big a church gets, it is still one church. It is not Trinity Saturday group, Trinity 8:30 group, Trinity Singles, Trinity this group, and Trinity that group. They're all a part of one body, and together they must make decisions concerning staff, money, schedules, music, and use of resources. And the closer the relationships across congregational lines, the more easily these decisions can be made.

However, this idea can be pressed too far. For one thing, it can sometimes ignore the fact that we all have only 168 hours a week. Consequently, no one can develop friendships with everyone in the church. If God answers our prayers and the church begins to grow rapidly, more people may join the church in any given quarter than anyone could really know as friends.

This may seem like a frail argument until we break the 168 hours down into available time. We all start with seven evenings a week. Perhaps you give two evenings to all-church activities. You devote an evening a week to your marriage and, if you have kids, an evening to the family. You spend one evening preparing your lesson, and some nights you make calls to newcomers or inactive members. You give Friday nights to Jesus. Finally, I'm sure many of you have other activities related to work, school, or occasional extra church meetings that tie up several evenings a month. If you have soccer-aged children, they will take about seven evenings a week.

The point is, when we get right down to counting evenings, we can't have or do it all. We must make some hard choices. Do we give ourselves to all-church activities, or do we devote ourselves to our group to the exclusion of other groups? We have to make a difficult choice. We can spend our limited time to strengthen relationships in the church, or we can intentionally create some relationships with outsiders.

The best response to an increasing pluralism is to celebrate, rather than bemoan, our diversity, to encourage the formation of new groups and loyalty to those groups. We will, of course, always need large group celebrations, but we must constantly work at "dividing" the church! I wish I had a dollar for every time someone has said, "Josh, you're trying to divide the church!" There is a sense in which this accusation is true. Guilty as charged. But that is how the body grows. The body does not grow by each cell getting bigger; it grows by strengthening and multiplying each and every cell.

Some have also objected that I'm not hard enough on cliques in the church. But the truth is, cliques aren't so bad when you're in one. In fact, this is the difference between a clique and a "close, warm, loving fellowship." If you are a member of the group, it is a close,

> *If I am already in a clique, I don't mind you being in one as well.*

135

warm, loving fellowship. But if you are on the outside, it's a clique. People who are in cliques don't complain. They love it there. It's the people on the outside who complain. Let me be clear. If I am already in a clique, I don't mind you being in one as well. I couldn't care less that your clique is closed to me. I don't want to be in your clique. I have a clique of my own. It is the people who are in no clique at all who complain. And these are the people the body needs to lovingly include in someone's group. Don't argue their point about cliques. Just love them. When they see the joy on the inside, they'll stop complaining and start rejoicing with you.

Of course, the word "clique" may also describe a group that is not open to anyone—a closed group. I, too, am deeply opposed to this kind of group. However, I have not found that nagging groups to be more inclusive is terribly effective. Just start more groups. New, and especially smaller, groups tend to be more inclusive. People who are in small, new groups have a hunger for new blood.

So how big should a group be before you divide it to form new groups? That is the wrong question. If you ask the wrong question, you are sure to get the wrong answer. There are no good answers to bad questions. Some better questions are:

● Do we want to reach our city for God?
● Do we believe in the principle of multiplication?
● Do we want to start new groups at all?
● How quickly can we start new groups?
● What is the best way for us to start a new group?

If they are well-organized, some groups can grow rather large and still function in a healthy way. It is more difficult to care for everyone in a large group, but it can be done. The best answer to the question "When do we have to reproduce new groups?" is "As soon as you can, as often as you can."

The high price of saying goodbye

Behind all the resistance to starting new groups lies a reality that is not well-understood. This reality is the high price of saying goodbye. Saying goodbye is one of the greatest sacrifices we will ever be called upon to make. For many, the price is just too high.

Do you know what keeps more missionaries off the mission field than anything else? It's not money or available personnel. The main obstacle that keeps would-be missionaries off the mission field is grand-parents. That's right—grandparents. Take it from a missionary's kid.

When my parents were preparing to go to the Philippines for the first time, they sat down to talk to their parents about the need, the possibilities, and their sense of calling to meet the need. My grandparents replied without stuttering, "No. You are not going to take our grandbabies halfway around the world to raise them among people who don't even wear shoes. You're not going to do it. We're not going to spend the next four Christmases without our grandchildren. We're not going to say goodbye to them and see them once every four years."

My parents went anyway, and we did not grow up with a close, loving relationship with our extended family. We barely knew many of our aunts and uncles. We didn't grow up playing with our cousins. When my uncle died in a farming accident, the entire family gathered for the funeral. The entire family, that is, except for one family. We were ten thousand miles away on the far side of the international date line. The price of saying goodbye is extremely high.

> *The price of saying goodbye is extremely high.*

When my sister was married, my parents weren't there to give her away. They watched their youngest daughter's wedding on video. They will never have the memory of being there in person. When my sons were born, my parents weren't here. They didn't see them until they were two. They have no memories of them learning to walk and uttering their first words. The price of saying goodbye is painfully high.

What does this have to do with small-group work? Everything. It's right here that groups stall in the process of doubling every two years or less. I'm afraid that many of us are simply unwilling to say goodbye.

I'm not asking you to move ten thousand miles to a different culture and climate. I'm not asking you to leave all your family and friends behind. I'm not asking you to miss your daughter's wedding or your grandchildren's births. But I *am* asking you to pay the price that missionaries pay, the high price of saying goodbye.

I *am* asking you to say goodbye to several of your friends. I am asking you to give up spending some evenings with them so you can spend those evenings with people who have no Christian friends. If we love them, they will come. But in order to make new friends for Jesus, we must be willing to say goodbye to some old friends. That's what giving Friday nights to Jesus is all about.

Write it down: Your friends will *not* understand, just as my grandparents didn't understand. They'll think you are snobbish and aloof. Feeling unloved, they might accuse you of being unloving. Be kind to them but firm in your resolve.

Now some good news. You don't have to say goodbye to all your friends, and you don't have to say goodbye completely or forever. I'm not asking you to move to Manila—just down the hall or to a different time. You can even take your three or four closest friends with you, and you can still see the others occasionally. I hope this lessens the pain.

> *Our future is in the multiplication of groups, so we should create a new unit every time we can.*

I also hope you understand that the pain is quite real and very deep. Saying goodbye is difficult. It is the highest price we pay in small-group work. Reproduction of a group is difficult on any level, but it's absolutely essential to the survival of the next generation. Our future is in the multiplication of groups, so we should create a new unit every time we can. The point of doubling is not to go from ten people to twenty but to go from one group to two, from two to four, from four to eight, and so on.

NOTES

[1] Lyle E. Schaller, *Assimilating New Members*, (Nashville, TN: Abingdon Press, 1978), 100.

Section Three:
Getting the Job Done

We can reach our nation for God through groups that are doubling every two years or less. We can do it by...

Teaching a halfway decent lesson,

Inviting every member and every prospect to every fellowship every month,

Giving Friday nights to Jesus,

Encouraging the group to ministry, and

Reproducing the group.

We can do it... if we have the right attitude. Attitude is everything.

Passion

My favorite verses in Romans are not 1:12; 3:23; 5:8; 6:23; 8:28; or 12:1. Those are all good verses, but my favorites are Romans 12:11-12: "Never be lacking in zeal, but keep your spiritual fervor, serving the Lord. Be joyful in hope, patient in affliction, faithful in prayer."

Our success in doubling our classes every two years or less may have more to do with these verses than with just about anything else. Sheer enthusiasm may not make the car run straight, but it will sure make it run fast. If you want to double your class in two years or less, you must have the energy that comes from the attitude of zeal.

I hate to admit it, but there are verses I'm not all that excited about. There are times when loving your neighbor is a drag. There are times when being submissive to authority is a pain. I wish, at times, that these commands were not in the Bible. But this command . . . I like this one.

I love being full of spiritual fervor and not lacking in zeal. This is what I want to be. If I could choose any mood to be in all the time, it would be continually fired up by and for God. It is then that what God wants of me is totally congruent with what I want to do. My will and God's lie parallel. We often think of our will and God's will as being at odds with each other, but it is often not the case. When I am full of spiritual zeal, my will and God's will are the same. I want to be full of zeal. Don't you?

Don't miss the fact that this is a command. To live a life full of spiritual zeal is just as much a command as the command to obey the government or love all people. It is a command. It is something that God wants us to do. Living a life of zeal is not only a joy to me, it is a command of God. This is something we need to take seriously.

At times, I must admit, I am less than full of spiritual fervor and zeal. At times I am bored and apathetic with Christian living. At times my heart doesn't throb with zeal for the Great Commission. At times I could best be described as sleepy. I need to repent and learn to be obedient to the command to stay full of zeal.

If I could stay full of zeal and never lack spiritual fervor . . .

- I would pray as I ought to pray.
- I would serve the Lord as I ought to serve the Lord.
- I would not be as tempted by sin as I sometimes am.

- I would get along with people better.
- I would be more eager to serve.
- I would be more loving with my family.
- I would double my class every two years or less.

Everything I want to do, every goal I want to reach would come nearer completion if I stayed obedient to this command. Motivation is 90 percent of almost everything. Everything goes better with zeal.

> *Everything I want to do, every goal I want to reach would come nearer completion if I stayed obedient to this command.*

Fortunately, Paul explains why we should and how we can stay full of zeal. You can see why these are my favorite verses. If being full of zeal is something I want, something I'm not, something that's 90 percent of almost everything, and the how-to is explained in these verses, what could be better?

Let me explain. After telling us what not to do (never lack zeal) and what to do (keep our spiritual fervor), Paul explains the purpose of our spiritual fervor. We are not to get happy just for the sake of getting happy. We are to get happy to get a job done, to serve the Lord. The purpose of our never lacking in zeal and always keeping spiritual fervor is to serve the Lord. Fulfilling the Great Commission is one way to serve the Lord, and doubling your class in two years or less is a worthy means toward that end. It's one example of serving the Lord.

So how do we maintain zeal to serve the Lord? Verse 12 spells it out: "Be joyful in hope, patient in affliction, faithful in prayer." Let's look at each of these in a little more detail.

Step one: Be joyful in hope.

Let me paraphrase this: "Be joyful in everything there is to be joyful in. Take full advantage of every joyful thing." Granted, every joy has a hidden sorrow. Every silver lining has a cloud. Look at the silver lining. Concentrate on the joy. Paul said something similar in Philippians 4:8: "Finally, brothers, whatever is true,

> *Every silver lining has a cloud. Look at the silver lining. Concentrate on the joy.*

whatever is noble, whatever is right, whatever is pure, whatever is lovely, whatever is admirable—if anything is excellent or praiseworthy—think about such things."

An example of this is found in Exodus 15. The people of Israel had just crossed the Red Sea. They had just experienced a marvelous victory, the end of over four hundred years of slavery. But there was still much to be done—a desert to cross, nations to conquer, and a land to possess. Miriam displays the kind of spirit Paul is describing when she sings: "Sing to the Lord, for he is highly exalted. The horse and its rider he has hurled into the sea" (Exodus 15:21). There is no mention of the desert yet to be crossed, no mention of the land still to be conquered, no mention of every depressing thought that could have been dreamed up. Miriam just wanted to rejoice in the Lord.

Some people have an uncanny ability to concentrate on the cloud's dark side rather than its silver lining. Don't do it. It will rob you of zeal. It will make you ineffective in serving the Lord. As much as possible, concentrate on what is positive. Ask yourself questions such as

● What is great about this?
● What is God doing today that is exciting?
● What did God tell me *this morning* that I didn't know before?

If you ask the right questions, you get the right answers. Be joyful in hope.

Step two: Be patient in affliction.

If we are going to remain full of spiritual zeal, our zeal can't depend upon circumstances. We must discover a source of zeal that will allow us to be patient in affliction. There's a popular theology that teaches that people's problems vanish with a prayer when they become Christians, that Christians have no more suffering or crying or tears or pain. However, that isn't what the Bible says. It teaches that Christians will have trouble in this world (John 16:33).

Therefore, we must learn to be full of zeal even in the middle of affliction. Consider the words of Peter: "Dear friends, do not be surprised at the painful trial you are suffering, as though something strange were happening to you. But rejoice that you participate in the sufferings of Christ, so that you may be overjoyed when his glory is revealed" (1 Peter 4:12-13).

Rejoicing that we participate in Christ's sufferings is one of the most difficult commands in the Bible. Only God can empower us to do it. But rejoicing in God and his hope during difficult days is one of the crowning marks of maturity.

Step three: Be faithful in prayer.

Most of us have heard convicting sermons on Revelation 3:16, which warns against being lukewarm. Often I've heard it preached, "You bad people—you're lukewarm!" I think a better sermon on this verse would explain how to be on fire for God. The truth is, I don't want to be lukewarm. I want to be on fire for God. I want to never lack zeal, to keep spiritual fervor, and to serve the Lord. But to do this, I must be faithful in prayer. What this means for me is a daily time of prayer with the Father. There is no substitute.

When I have substantial, unhurried, quality time with the Lord in prayer and in his Word, my life is full of zeal...no matter what is going on. There's a one-to-one relationship between the two. When my time with God is on, zeal is on. When time with God is off, zeal is off. It's just that simple.

> *When I have substantial, unhurried, quality time with the Lord in prayer and in his Word, my life is full of zeal ... no matter what is going on.*

But don't make a quiet time a matter of law. The law principle will never make real Christian disciples. It won't fill us with zeal. Only people who pray because they know the privilege of prayer will be full of zeal.

Do you know how often I pray? Only when I feel like praying. Honestly. I pray and read my Bible only when I feel like it. If I don't feel like it, I don't do it. So how often do I pray? How often do I read my Bible? Not as much as I would like. I'd love to do more. But I pray and read just about every day because I feel like praying and reading my Bible almost every day.

It may take a little while to form the habit of a consistent daily time with God, but never forget that it is a matter of grace, not law. There is no place for condemnation in Christianity. We get to have a quiet time; we don't have to. The point is not that we pray out of a sense of obligation. The point is that we delight ourselves in the Lord.

We will never reach our nation for God with bored and apathetic Christians. We will never reach our communities with anything less than Christians who are on fire for God. No matter how good our methods, we will be a car without fuel if we are not living lives of all-out zeal for God.

So take a moment right now to ask God to help you turn from your apathy and to empower you to be obedient to the command to ...

be joyful in hope,
patient in affliction,
faithful in prayer.

How to Get Things Done

Surely by now you've been asking yourself, "How in the world can I do all that I need to do? I have a family, I need to spend quite a few hours preparing the lesson, I have other church responsibilities, work is demanding more and more time, and on and on and on..."

The short answer is to cut out some things. Find out what you are good at, and do it well. Here's a slogan that's worth the price of this book: one person, one job. Churches should adopt this slogan as their guiding principle in recruiting people to ministry. If you are involved in fourteen responsibilities at church, cut out some things.

You have probably seen a performer trying to balance a number of plates. Taking one plate and a long stick, the performer spins the plate and balances it on the stick. Then he takes a second plate and starts it spinning—then a third, a fourth, and so on until the first plate begins to slow down. The performer runs to the first plate and keeps it spinning and, after starting yet another plate, speeds up the second and third plates. Soon he is running back and forth trying to keep all these plates balanced.

That is a perfect picture of modern life—running to and from work, home, soccer, church, this and that, trying to keep all our plates balanced. At times we just want to let them all crash. If that is how you feel, this chapter is for you.

> *For a Christian, time management can be reduced to a simple formula: Figure out what God wants you to do, and then do it.*

I want to share some important principles for managing your time, for doing what you need to do. You can't do it all, but you can do enough. You may not be able to do everything that your boss, your spouse, or anyone else would like you to do. But you can do everything that God wants you to do. For a Christian, time management can be reduced to a simple formula: Figure out what God wants you to do, and then do it. That's it. God only demands 168 hours a week, and he realizes that in that time we must rest, get dressed, eat, work, get stuck in traffic, and have a million interruptions. I believe the following principles can help us control our calendars and schedules so we can do all that God wants us to do.

Say "no" once a day, just to keep in practice.

Come to grips with your humanity. You can't do it all, so accept it. You will have to leave some things undone. Get in touch with that. Get used to it. Learn to live with it. To survive, you must be able to look need in the face and say, "Not this time."

Decide what is important to you.

What do you want to do with your one and only life? What are you here for? What are your objectives? What do you want to get done? When you look back

> *What do you want to do with your one and only life?*

over your life, what do you want to see? For some, it is to house the homeless; for others, it is to legislate against abortion. For me, it is to take America for God by helping small-group leaders double their classes every two years or less. What do you want to do?

Set aside blocks of time for dreaming, strategizing, and evaluating.

Although it may feel as though you're really not doing anything, think time isn't wasted time. In fact, it may be the most important time you spend. The problem with the plate-balancing routine is that there's never time to step back and ask, "Why do I want these plates spinning, anyway?" You are simply too busy balancing plates to ask such questions. The easiest way to correct this is to schedule time to reflect, to dream, and to plan.

In spite of what you may be thinking, dreaming, strategizing, and evaluating *are* work. They are *doing* something. If, like me, you are a hands-on type, this is hard to grasp. We think dreaming is a waste of time. How can you be working when your feet are up on the desk? But in reality, the only way to live according to priorities is to set aside regular blocks of time for reflection. You can't do this while you're dictating memos, faxing documents, or washing dishes. You can't do it in blocks of ten minutes here and fifteen minutes there. You need unhurried and uninterrupted quality time to dream, to plan, and to evaluate effectively.

Never look back on a decision, except to learn from it.

The other day my family rode our bikes to the grocery store to get some milk and a few other items. On the way home, the groceries fell off. I told Sharon, "Sure, we should have strapped them on better; we made a poor decision—but no use crying over spilled milk." It really was just milk.

All too often we slow ourselves down by focusing on the "what ifs," the "should haves," and the "if onlys." Of course we could have made a better decision if we knew then what we know now. But we didn't, so we made a less than perfect decision. That's that. But no use crying over spilled milk. Forgetting what is behind and reaching toward what is ahead, let's press on (see Philippians 3:13).

Realize that it is futility, more than work, that wearies the soul.

Contrary to popular belief, we are not allergic to work. It's good for us. Luke 5:1-11 records the story of the disciples fishing all night. At the end of the night, they were exhausted. But it doesn't seem that working all night tired them as much as working all night and catching nothing. When we enjoy the adrenaline of fruitful labor for God, we can work and work and work. The joy of the Lord will be our strength (Nehemiah 8:10).

> *We are not allergic to work, so we should not shirk it.*

We are not allergic to work, so we should not shirk it. Jesus said, "My food [what satisfies and nourishes me] is to do the will of him who sent me and to finish his work" (John 4:34). Jesus' food was God's work. The thing that wearies the soul is the feeling of not accomplishing anything significant. One of the truths I want you to take from this book is that, when you give yourself to doubling your class every two years, you are giving yourself to a worthy work. It should satisfy you, not exhaust you.

Block out time for personal and family recreation.

The flip side is: Don't work all the time. We all need time to recharge our batteries. We all need to rest. Block out chunks of time to rest and devote yourself fully to personal and family recreation. When you rest, rest hard. When you work, work hard. When you play, play hard. Whatever you do, be fully engaged. Colossians 3:23 states, "Whatever you do, work at it with all your heart, as working for the Lord, not for men."

The best antidote to drivenness is obedience to the fourth of the Ten Commandments, the Sabbath command. Taking one solid day to rest and to worship revives the soul as nothing else does. Sometimes church activities get in the way of obedience to the fourth command. (This is especially true if your paycheck has a church's name on it.) Find a way to be obedient. It will do you good. Sunday is not a day of rest for pastors, so they need to take some other day off. A morning here and an afternoon there simply will not do. Nothing will increase our productivity like doing nothing for one day.

Occasionally people get confused on the priority of family and ministry. There is no conflict of interest. You never have to choose between family and ministry. Your first ministry *is* to your family, then to the rest of the world. Everything we do is ministry. We minister to God in worship and prayer. We minister to our children by building blocks with them. We minister by taking our spouses out for dinner and a movie. We minister when we teach. We minister when we give Friday nights to Jesus. It's all ministry.

Hang around people who fire you up.

Enthusiasm is contagious. As much as you can, hang around people who have it. It would be nice to be around enthusiastic people all the time, but this is as unrealistic as it is attractive. What we can do, however, is to find ourselves a few positive friends who will spur us on toward love and good deeds (Hebrews 10:24). Two good friends who will serve as your cheerleaders can make a world of difference. Boxers don't need a crowd in their corners, but we all need a few people. Who do you have in your corner?

> *Enthusiasm is contagious. As much as you can, hang around people who have it.*

Watch for energy leaks.

Watch out for people, things, projects, or influences that take the wind out of your sails. The Bible tells us to "never be lacking in zeal," and we need to take this command seriously. So the next time someone starts to exhaust your zeal, just think to yourself, "You're tempting me to disobey Romans 12:11. I am outta here."

Energy leaks come in various forms. They can be projects or people. Perhaps certain chores such as mowing the lawn or changing the oil in the car drive you nuts. Can you hire it done? Is it really worth what it costs you *emotionally* to save a few dollars doing it yourself? Other energy leaks are VDPs—very draining people. Avoid them when you can. We need to watch out for and avoid projects and people that wear us down.

Think ahead.

In a word: plan. You'll usually be able to work smarter if you think ahead. Group similar tasks together. Ask people about things when you see them rather than making extra calls to do it. Take care of all three errands at once and avoid a second trip. This saves time and demonstrates leadership. The mark of a leader is someone who is always ahead of the group. With a leader's guidance, a group can sit down in one evening and plan out the activities for an entire semester. In fact, if people are really motivated, they can plan an entire year's calendar in one evening. Planning saves time.

Do what you want to do when you want to do it.

> *Most people recommend that you do the most important jobs first. I disagree.*

Most people recommend that you do the most important jobs first. I disagree. While this may be best in some cases, it doesn't always work best. Let's say you have a list of six things to do, and all of them have to be done. All other things being equal, you'll do them better and more quickly if you do each task when you feel like it. Of course, this principle assumes that you'll eventually feel like doing what you need to do, which is a reasonably valid assumption.

I love variety. Sometimes I like to plan. Sometimes I enjoy working with my hands. Often I love to study, but other times I am energized by dreaming. At times I like to be with people; at times I need to be alone. I'm sure you have your own list of things that have to be done. As much as possible, do what you want to do when you want to do it. You will accomplish more and enjoy life more. Also, your motivation will stay higher, and motivation is 90 percent of almost everything.

Delegate.

The easiest way to save time and accomplish a great deal is to get other people involved in the work you're doing. Delegation is part of the disciple-making process. You see, your class members need to work too. They need to be trusted, supported, and set free to serve. Take the risk, even when you could do a better job, and trust others with parts of the work. They need to feel that they own of a part of God's work.

Remember Nehemiah 3—that long list of hard-to-pronounce names of the people who rebuilt the Jerusalem wall? (So and so rebuilt the wall from here to there; next to him, so and so rebuilt the wall up to the Sheep Gate...) Each person was responsible for a part of the wall. Nehemiah couldn't do it by himself, and neither can you.

In addition, giving people something to do makes them feel a part of the group. One of the greatest needs of most churches is assimilating new members. There are generally two ways people become assimilated: they make six friends, or they become involved in the work. My friend Jeff Wagner has told me that a pivotal part in his process of becoming involved in the church was my asking him to be in charge of Bible distribution. I needed someone to help, and he did a great job. More important, helping with the work did something for him. He was forever assimilated into the life of the body. Do not be afraid to ask people to help.

Give trivial time to trivial work.

Sometimes in life we get to deal with the grand and glorious. Sometimes we have to thumb through mail. There is nothing glorious or glamorous about mail, but sooner or later it has to be done. There are times to explore the riches of God's Word, to help class members discover new truth, to handle holy things. Then the floor needs to be mopped, the phone calls returned, and the refreshments purchased. This is life on planet Earth. Give your best time—when you are full of spiritual zeal—to the most important tasks. But when you are idling along at a quiet hum, give yourself to mundane matters, and get the mundane out of the way.

Don't spend any more time on a task than the task is worth. Handle mail once. It's too easy to put all your junk in a pile and then rearrange the pile once a week. At my house, we have boxes of stuff that we've done nothing but rearrange through four moves. They sit in the garage, waiting for us to rearrange them each spring. As much as possible, reduce the clutter in your life. Simplify. Throw some things away. Ask yourself, "What's the worst that will happen if I forget about this?" If the answer is "Nothing all that bad," forget it. Then get back to the grand

and glorious task of being obedient to the Great Commission.

Keep a list of time squeezers.

Time squeezers are things you can squeeze into an extra five minutes here and there. For example,

- never be without a book.
- never be without some Scripture memory to review.
- listen to tapes as you drive.
- worship whenever you have a spare moment.

Caution: If you push this idea too far, we will color you driven. Remember to take time for personal and family relaxation.

Organize for productivity.

The test of organization is this: Does it help me get the work done? It doesn't matter how pretty the organizational scheme may be. The question is, does it help to get the work done?

When I was growing up, we employed a housecleaner who had a bad habit of cleaning the top of my dad's desk. She would organize it all in neat little piles—so much so that Dad would be unable to find anything and became half as productive as he would have been if left alone. He was better organized . . . but less productive. He was also irritated.

Organization can help, however. For example, I keep my keys in about six different places, and every morning I have to check all six places to find them. In this case, lack of organization is hurting me. If you spend ten minutes searching through a pile of papers every day, it would be far more efficient to spend some time filing them in some way. But you may want to start by throwing half the pile away.

If you start working on your lesson early, your subconscious will prepare half of it while you do other things.

Get started on your lesson early.

If you start working on your lesson early, your subconscious will prepare half of it while you do other things. So give your mind time to collect ideas, find illustrations, and allow all your thoughts to simmer. The mind is a wonderful machine. If, early in the week, you carefully read through the Scripture your lesson will be based upon, the lesson will be half-written by the end of the week.

Read.

Regular reading will help you in more ways than you probably realize. When Paul was in prison, he asked Timothy to bring him his "scrolls, especially the parchments" (2 Timothy 4:13). Scrolls were, of course, the ancient equivalent of books. Books were important to Paul. Books have always been important to God's people. Books are a tremendous source of information and illustrations. So instead of reading another commentary, read James Dobson, C.S. Lewis, or Max Lucado. It will add depth and color to your lessons. You'll become a more interesting person to listen to.

Reevaluate regularly.

No plan or approach will set you up for life. Life is constantly changing, and we must constantly adjust to meet its changing needs. I don't know how the church got in the shape it's in. I don't pretend to have all the answers for getting us out. But I do know one thing: We must change. Even if we fail, at least we will have learned some things.

I am a card-carrying member of the "one hundred ideas a year" club. I am constantly coming up with ideas. Unfortunately, most of them aren't very good. I try many of them, and I regularly fail. But I'm not discouraged. In fact, I would like to fail and recover faster and more often. Trial and error is a marvelous teacher. Remember, the core meaning of "disciple" is "learner."

Life is filled with so many competing time demands that we'll never be able to double our groups every two years or less without carefully managing our lives. These ideas for managing time will help you start. What one change in the way you manage your time do you need to make right now?

Laziness, Ignorance, Failure, and Thievery

To appreciate the depth of insight in this chapter, you'll have to observe my tongue firmly planted in my cheek. I have read more than one hundred books on church growth. After a while, they all start to sound the same. So, to gain fresh insight, I began reading secular (even humanistic) management, sales, and marketing books. I found some truth in these books and continue to read them with pleasure and profit. Some of their ideas, of course, are totally incongruent with biblical teaching and must be discarded. But many ideas are readily adaptable to Christian ministry. They're just good common sense.

I want to talk to you about four principles or values I've gained from these books: laziness, ignorance, failure, and thievery. I think the devil has had these ideas long enough. It's time to reclaim them and put them to good use.

> *One of our problems is that we work too hard, sweat too much, and labor too diligently.*

Laziness

One of our problems is that we work too hard, sweat too much, and labor too diligently. Jethro taught us that the work ought to be getting easier. The cookies don't go to the ones who work hard; they go to the ones who get plenty done. We too easily confuse busyness with productivity. We desperately need to cultivate laziness.

We cultivate laziness by giving the ministry away. There's a great tendency to control the ministry, to have our hands on every part of the work. We tend to believe that we can do things better than others, that perhaps no one else can do it quite as well as we can. (It may be true, but only because we have been at it longer than those around us.) We know the feelings of self-esteem and worth we get when we do a job well. We *want* to feel needed and important, but we *need* to cultivate laziness.

Instead of doing the work of ten people, we need to put ten people to work. Not only does it allow them to grow, it helps us to keep our priorities straight. It enables us to meet important needs such as quiet time and family time. It allows all God's work to be done with excellence.

Never turn down an offer for help. Every now and then (it won't happen often) someone will ask, "Anything I can do to help?" The answer to that question is always "YES!" You can answer questions about how and when later. Nothing demotivates people like being turned down when they finally work up the courage to offer to help. Think about how you would feel if someone told you, "Yeah, I know you would like to help, but I can't think of a cotton-picking thing that someone like you could do!" Now that would put wind in your sails, wouldn't it?

We need to cultivate laziness in another area. We need to be ruthlessly pragmatic about how we do things. Never do something the hard way when the easy way will do. Howard Hendricks tells the story of a missionary who used to spend three days canoeing to a remote village to share the gospel with the people there. One day, Mission Aviation Fellowship told him, *Never do something the hard way when the easy way will do.* "We can fly you there in three hours." "No thanks," he replied, "this is what I'm called to do." But what *was* he called to do: to canoe or to fulfill the Great Commission?

I'm a great fan of using every available means of conserving time and energy. So can you. How can you use fax machines, e-mail, cellular phones, and the Internet to make you more productive? How can you save time by making phone calls instead of unnecessary personal visits? We are not called to activity—we are called to help get a job done. Therefore, we must be ruthlessly pragmatic about our effectiveness in the most important endeavor known to humanity. We must work smarter, not harder.

For example, I once spent a summer in Farmington, New Mexico, helping a church get started. I personally rapped my knuckles against one thousand doors. Later, during a telemarketing campaign, I made nearly as many contacts in one week as I had made in ten weeks of knocking on doors, with about the same results. Needless to say, we began making much heavier use of the telephone to contact visitors, new members, people who needed to be assimilated, and people who seemed to be drifting. We began cultivating laziness.

Of course, sometimes a face-to-face visit is necessary—when you're sharing the gospel, for example. But sometimes a visit is resented. It's seen as a pestering intrusion of privacy. So visit when you need to, but call when a call will do. When you do visit, set up an appointment so you know your time will be used wisely. I encourage you to make ten times as many calls as you do visits. Don't make a visit unless it's the only way to get done what you want to get done. Work smarter, not harder. Cultivate laziness.

Finally, a word about lesson preparation. My friend Ken Woods once asked, "How much should I study for my Sunday school lesson?" My response: "As little as possible!" You need to prepare a quality lesson every week, something that is biblical, practical, positive, clear, and interesting. But you do not need to say that you spent so many hours in preparation. It's not how hard you work; it's what you get done. Excellence in teaching is the point, not logging hours. If you can prepare a halfway decent lesson in two hours, don't spend four. Use the other two hours to call every member of your class just to tell them you are interested in what is going on in their lives. Work smarter, not harder. Cultivate laziness. It is a key to doubling your class.

> *It is the ignorant who are hungry for knowledge.*

Ignorance

Laziness, ignorance, failure, and thievery—four bedrocks of church growth.

How does ignorance contribute to the growth of a class? Much in every way! It is the ignorant who are hungry for knowledge. They approach every lesson as if they have never seen it before. Aware of their ignorance, they study with an abandonment to fatigue. They dive in after every detail.

The ignorant have a similar hunger to discover better ways of doing things. They never assume that they have arrived at the best way. They know they're ignorant. They constantly read, reevaluate, and try new approaches. They draw lessons from every area of life and apply them to their classes.

The ignorant are humble. When you talk to them, they listen. They hang intently on every word. They know they're ignorant—they long to know more.

The ignorant will try just about anything. They don't know any better. They just try it. Who cares if they've never done it that way before? It might work. Who knows? Not the ignorant.

All too many experts know all kinds of reasons we cannot reach our nation and world for God. With computer analyses and impressive graphs, they offer intelligent-sounding, logical reasons we cannot do what God told us to do. They feel more than a little cynical about the kind of optimism found in this book. Many of them are smarter than I am.

But I know this: God left us with a job to do. I expect that he means business. When my mama gave me chores to do while she was out of the house, she meant business. I know this as well: You can double your group by inviting every member and every prospect to every fellowship every week. You can reach your community for God through groups that are doubling every two years or less.

Work this week on cultivating ignorance. It can help your class double in the next two years.

Failure

If you want your class to grow, you must adopt four essential values: laziness, ignorance, failure, and thievery. This section explains how people who fail make great leaders, while people who never fail never grow

> *Anything worth doing is worth doing less than perfectly at first.*

classes. Anything worth doing is worth doing less than perfectly at first.

Lucille Ball's high school drama teacher told her she had no talent, that she would never make it, that she was a failure. Yet "Lucille Ball" is a household name fifty years later. And the drama teacher—who ever heard of her? Apparently, Lucille Ball knew you have to fail to succeed. We need to learn that too.

One of the major themes of the Bible is that failure is not final. We can risk failure because we know that God is a God of second chances, and we can recover from failure because we know that God forgives and restores.

> *One of the major themes of the Bible is that failure is not final.*

Perhaps there was a time in your life when you sought to do great things for God ... but failed miserably. Maybe you decided that it's easier to quit dreaming than to keep failing. I have good news. Failure is not final. I invite you to become a dreamer again. Dream with me about a better nation and a better world. Dream with me about being part of the army that makes it happen.

Consider the story of Jonah. God called Jonah to a missionary ministry in Nineveh, capital city of Assyria, Israel's most hated enemy. When Jonah disobeyed God, he ended up in the belly of a fish, with seaweed wrapped around his face. I suspect that Jonah felt like a failure. To be honest, he was a failure at this point. But failure is not final—God is a God of second chances—and Jonah eventually made his way to Nineveh and announced God's message to the people there.

Because we are secure in our relationship with Christ, because we know God will forgive us when we need it, because we know God believes in us—we can risk failure. I encourage you to try something that may not work. You never know. It just may work. I would never have bet that we could sustain a Bible study group meeting at 7:30 Sunday mornings. But it worked. In fact, it met a tremendous need and increased the options we can offer to the community. But the point is—it might have failed. No one knew for sure. Only those who risk failure have the opportunity to receive great rewards. You can't steal second base with your foot on first. In order to discover new oceans, you have to lose sight of the shore.

I've heard people say that they never fail because, when they pray, they receive clear guidance from God. Following God for me, however, has been more a process of trying and failing. I've planned a number of programs that missed the target. They were not well-attended. They didn't meet needs. They cost time, energy, and money without reaching their objectives. We failed.

> *I believe God is more pleased when we risk and fail than when we never risk any-thing at all.*

But life goes on. God forgives. In fact, I believe God is more pleased when we risk and fail than when we never risk anything at all. We learn some new things and become better at others. If we try the same old approaches over and over and over again, we'll never learn, we'll never get better. If we keep doing what we have been doing, we are going to keep getting what we have been getting.

If you've failed in the past, chin up. God forgives. If you haven't failed, point your skis downhill. You'll never really learn to ski until you push yourself forward and occasionally fall down. Try some better ways of ministering to your class members and prospects. If your methods fail, remember: Life goes on. Failure is not final. God is a God of second chances.

Thievery

Laziness, ignorance, and failure are important, but you also need to cultivate thievery.

Recently my friend Mike Draper told me that there are three types of football coaches: innovators, thieves, and the unemployed. He admitted that he's no innovator, but he still has a job. In fact, he and his team are doing quite well. His secret? He is a skillful thief! Similarly, Rick Warren says, "If my bullet fits in your gun, shoot it." With that in mind, I freely admit that there is hardly a thing in this book I didn't steal!

There is hardly a thing in this book I didn't steal!

Don't make the same stubborn mistake as the man who said he would be original or nothing. He ended up being both. You'll probably never be able to come up with enough original ideas to do your job adequately. It's much easier (and much smarter) to be a thief. That's the attitude with which I hope you read this book—not to slavishly follow every detail but to gain ideas.

Humans love two things: change and consistency. We love the seasons because each one is different and yet they are always the same. Your class loves variety, too, and they'll get bored if you're not giving them some new ideas. Where do you get those ideas?

You steal them.

I've stolen ideas from a wide variety of places. For example, I stole ideas about disciple-making from the Navigators. Similarly, I'm not an evangelist, so I've stolen from people who have written books on evangelism. My most productive source of ideas has been the whole school of church growth. Leadership books have proven enormously useful. I started with books on Christian leadership and then crossed the bridge to secular books on worldly leadership. I am now embezzling from the account of marketing books. The point is—all these ideas are lying out in the open, with no lock or key. They are just begging to be stolen.

But enough about me. Who are you stealing from? What's the last book you read that really stretched you? Have you uncovered any new ideas within unlikely sources lately? Have you stolen anything recently?

If you want to double your class every two years or less, find out where you can steal good ideas. Cultivate laziness by giving the ministry away. Be humble enough to accept your ignorance and stay hungry to learn. And if you fail, remember God's grace.

"Apart From Me You Can Do Nothing"

The danger of being optimistic is that it's too easy to forget the truth of John 15:1-5. The branch can only produce fruit if it's connected to the vine. It doesn't matter what the branch produced last year. All that matters is that it's connected to the vine today. God has had to thoroughly break many people to ensure that they did not forget this truth.

It's for this reason that I am almost ritualistic about praying the following prayer. We pray it at least once a week:

> Father, we confess our awareness that it is not by might and not by power but by your Spirit. We confess our awareness that without you we can do nothing. You are the source of all blessing. You are the changer of lives. It is you who is drawing all people to yourself. Nothing of true spiritual or lasting value comes without you. Father, humbly but confidently we confess our strong confidence in you. We confess our strong confidence that you are a God of miracles, a God who can change lives, a God who specializes in the impossible.

We are tempted to think, foolish as it sounds, that we changed people's lives.

When God blesses our work, we fall victim to a whole set of new temptations that didn't affect us before. We are tempted by pride as we were not before. We are tempted to think, foolish as it sounds, that we changed people's lives. We are tempted to believe that, if we will simply follow steps one, two, and three, we can double our classes with or without God's blessing.

Danger! Beware! Remember, Jesus said, "Apart from me you can do nothing."

My father, who taught at a Bible school, used to trick his students with this question: True or false? Jesus said that without him we can accomplish very little.

How would you answer that question? There is only one right answer. False. Jesus did not say that we can accomplish very little without him. We like to think that's what he said. In fact, we like to think that we can accomplish quite a bit without him. We admit that we could do more with him, but we would like to believe that we can accomplish something on our own.

Wrong.

Jesus taught that we can accomplish nothing of true, lasting, or spiritual value without abiding in him. The Bible also teaches that God opposes the proud (James 4:6). So, those who minister without abiding in the vine end up in opposition to God. The other side is also true: God is more than willing to bless his children who do his work for his glory. God is not stingy in passing out his blessings.

If you want to double your class every two years or less, rest assured that it will involve far more than programs and numbers. It's not just about giving Friday nights to Jesus and inviting every member and every prospect to every fellowship every month. There are deeply spiritual issues at stake. We must abide in the vine if we are to see *any* lasting, spiritual fruit.

The Other Side of Success

I believe the ideas presented in this book will help you reach and disciple many people for Christ. I believe they will enable your class to grow more rapidly than ever before. I believe they will work for you as you apply them through the personality and temperament God has given you. I believe that these ideas are biblically sound. But I recognize that, for every truth in Scripture, there is an equal and balancing truth. For example, the Bible teaches that...

God is one—God is three

People are chosen by God—People are responsible to God

We should obey our spiritual authority—Every believer is a priest

We are totally accepted by God—No one is righteous before God

We must work—We must rest

We must work as if it all depended upon us—We must pray as if it all depended upon God

With that in mind, I want to balance everything I've said to this point with what I have to say in this chapter. I want to talk to you about "the other side of success."

The idea hit me in a rather pointed way when we conducted our telemarketing campaign. I was knee-deep in telemarketing, making a hundred calls every day, coordinating teams of callers, and arranging places and phones to contact hundreds of homes every day. During my quiet time one morning, I read, "Make it your ambition to lead a quiet life, to mind your own business and to work with your hands, just as we told you" (I Thessalonians 4:11).

God's timing is hilarious! Somehow my mind couldn't quite reconcile making a hundred unsolicited calls a day with leading a quiet life and minding my own business. Yet I knew that what we were doing was working better than anything else we had ever done. We were fulfilling the Great Commission. The real question for me was not how to reconcile telemarketing with leading a quiet life but how to reconcile minding my own business with making disciples of all nations.

I can no more reconcile these commands in my head than I can fully

160

comprehend the truths at the beginning of this chapter. Still, my heart can reconcile these commands, even if my head can't. In fact, these two seemingly incompatible truths have gotten along rather well in the inner sanctum of my heart. There is a quiet place within me where they coexist as friends.

Perhaps they coexist because of the journey God has taken me on during the past several months. On this journey I revisited Psalm 127:2 ("In vain you rise early and stay up late, toiling for food to eat—for he grants sleep to those he loves") and Ecclesiastes 4:6 ("Better one handful with tranquillity than two handfuls with toil"). This journey helped me rediscover such novel ideas as a date night with Sharon and a day off each week. This journey led me toward a slower, less driven, less frenzied life, because I am in it for the long haul. I am still eager, enthusiastic, diligent, and (hopefully) never lacking in zeal. But now I am just as excited (not just obligated) to put blocks together with Dustin and watch Dawson play soccer as I am to put together the new 2020 Vision World Wide Web site.

It's humbling to realize that Jesus, who was full of spiritual zeal and who had the most demanding job in all of history, was never frenzied or stressed. My head can no more reconcile "zeal" with "a quiet life" than it can comprehend God's mercy and wrath. But in my heart there is a quiet, open place where they coexist. I cannot hold deer in a quiet meadow and enjoy their beauty, but if I rest quietly and watch, they do not run. In the same way, I cannot hold zeal for the Great Commission together with a quiet life of minding my own business. But I find that if I let them go to the quiet meadow in my heart, they do not collide; they peacefully coexist. I watch in wonder at the beauty of God's truth.

> *It's humbling to realize that Jesus, who was full of spiritual zeal and who had the most demanding job in all of history, was never frenzied or stressed.*

Late in his life, an anonymous friar in a Nebraska monastery wrote:

If I had my life to live over again,
I'd try to make more mistakes next time.
I would relax, I would limber up,
I would be sillier than I have been this trip.
I would take more trips. I would be crazier.
I would climb more mountains, swim more rivers, and watch more sunsets.
I would do more walking and looking.

I would eat more ice cream and less beans.
If I had it to do over again I would go places, do things, and travel lighter.
If I had my life to live over I would start barefooted earlier in the spring
    and stay that way later in the fall.
I would ride on more merry-go-rounds.
I'd pick more daisies.[1]

This is the other side of success: Slow down. If this message doesn't mean anything to you and you can't really relate to what I'm saying, you probably need to read it again.

> *God is never in favor of getting the work done at the expense of the worker.*

God is never in favor of getting the work done at the expense of the worker. He loves you so much that he doesn't want you to burn out. Granted, God wants you to get the work done, but so do you. God also wants to see you working twenty years from now. I want you to double your class as quickly as you can, but more important, I want to encourage you to protect the goose that lays the golden egg. If we lose you in the process, we will have lost too much. It's far better to double every five years and stay with it than to double in two years and burn out.

I love working with small groups. I love the conversations, the questions, the friends, the laughter, the tears, and the parties. I love every part of it. I want you to love it, too. I want you to love growing a group and doubling it every two years or less. I want you to love inviting every member and every prospect to every fellowship every month. I want you to love giving Friday nights to Jesus. I want you to love pouring yourself into a Timothy and then watching your group reproduce. So don't just do it. Love it.

NOTES

[1] Quoted in Alan Loy McGinnis, *Confidence* (Minneapolis, MN: Augsburg, 1987), 57-58.

What's It All About, Anyway?

I close with a story that illustrates what small-group life and Sunday school is all about. It's not about programs and institutions and activities and things you ought to do. It's about life. It's about how you spend your days and weekends. And it's about what happens to you when the storms of life come. You might want to grab a box of Kleenex. This chapter is dedicated to the memory of Kevin Davidson.

You might want to grab a box of Kleenex. This chapter is dedicated to the memory of Kevin Davidson.

The story begins on Mother's Day. While most of us were opening flowery Mother's Day cards, making long-distance phone calls, or going out to Sunday dinner, Sharon Davidson was at the hospital with little Kevin. This wasn't the first time she had held her child in a hospital bed, and it wouldn't be the last. Little Kevin, age five, had epilepsy, a rare form of epilepsy that would eventually take his life. Sharon and her husband, Don, had spent many a day at the hospital together with their son.

Sharon was a nurse, a skilled and loving professional who enjoyed caring for people. But no one ever got the care that little Kevin received. She put her best skills as a nurse to his service. She examined every prescription, double-checked every procedure. She asked questions to the point of exhaustion, explored every avenue, and pursued every "What if?" Sharon, like other mothers, cared for all her children, all four of them. But God gave her the special skill of a nurse to give Kevin the special care that he needed.

Don, Kevin's dad, was an auto mechanic, a rough and tough kind of guy with big shoulders and strong hands. But Don also had a tender heart, and little Kevin worked his way deeply into Daddy's heart.

Little Kevin worked his way into all our hearts. We loved him. We loved his courage, his smile. We saw him hurting, and we felt for his pain.

Sadly, Kevin's condition grew gradually worse throughout the summer. I took several trips up to Albuquerque to be with Sharon, Don, and Kevin. I watched as Don and Sharon held him hour after hour. I saw him hooked up to every tube and contraption known to medical science.

One day in late October, little Kevin took a nap. He woke up in the arms of Jesus. We often think that sickness will prepare us for death, but it never does. Death always seems unnatural because we were born for eternity. We have eternity in our hearts. We are fish out of water living in the finite.

Modern science is really something. Although Kevin was dead, the doctors started him breathing again. They did all they could to revive him. I suspect Sharon knew better, but I can't help but think that they revived her hopes. They gave him every chance, but it was just too late.

To say that we were all shocked by the news of Kevin's death is to state the obvious. But no one was as shocked as Sharon and Don. Sharon, who had dealt with death countless times in her work, was facing the death of her own son. Nothing in her training or experience had prepared her for this. Nothing could.

Our church was between pastors at that time, so the staff—Gary, Bill, and I—went to stand where the pastor normally stands. It is the pastor who normally stands on the front line in this kind of situation. That day we realized how far it is from our offices to the pastor's office. We went through the process of the funeral and the burial. We all handled it as best we could. Time passed. Life went on.

The part of the story I really want you to hear happened later, at our annual Christmas party. It was that time of month to invite every member and every prospect to our fellowship. This month we had planned a Christmas party, and the party-planners had gone all out. They had planned an elaborate Secret Santa gift exchange that went on for weeks before. We gave secret gifts to each other. Some of the gifts were more pranks than presents. On this night we would all find out who our Secret Santas were. Everyone seemed to be in a good mood that night. There was lots of laughter, backslapping, and joke-telling all around.

Unnoticed to the rest of the group, Sharon Davidson and Kim Wagner were off to one side talking. Kim is one of those motherly types who make good inreach leaders. Care comes naturally for her. Kim was making conversation with Sharon, as you do at Christmas parties, so she asked, "Sharon, do you have your decorations up?" Sharon began to cry. (As I am now. I have told this story dozens of times, and I have yet to do so without crying.) "No," Sharon replied softly. She paused, trying to hold back her tears, then said, "No, I don't. I know I should. The other kids need me to put the decorations up, but I just can't bring myself to do it. It's Christmas. Kevin should be here, but he's not. He will never be here again. We'll never see him for another Christmas. We will never, ever see Kevin again. How can I celebrate at a time like this? How can I ever celebrate anything?" Sharon and Kim held each other and cried.

Right there in that moment, Kim represented God to Sharon. She let her grieve. She let her cry. She told her she was sorry. And when Sharon was ready for the conversation to go on to something else, that was OK with Kim as well.

So the conversation (and the party) did go on. We talked of Secret Santas and Christmas plans and about how we were going to surprise the kids. The guys talked about bowl games and football playoffs and other such manly things. But behind the scenes, while all this was going on, Kim started passing a secret. She passed it from one person to the next, especially among the ladies, who then told their husbands. She told us all to wait around after the party. We needed to do something for Don and Sharon. We didn't know what. We just knew that there is a time for love to listen and a time for love to act. This was a time to act.

> *We just knew that there is a time for love to listen and a time for love to act. This was a time to act.*

Pooling our money, we gathered about $125. Then we all drove down to an all-night grocery store and bought a tree and decorations. Finally, at about eleven o'clock that night, we surprised Don, Sharon, and their three kids with our Christmas gift: "We understand that your souls are grieving for your absent child. We understand that there is nothing in you that wants to celebrate. We understand that you feel you may never celebrate anything ever again. But we want to help. We have come to decorate your home. We have come to help you celebrate." And all the way until midnight, we had a party decorating Sharon and Don's house.

I have a feeling that, years from now, when Sharon and Don are asked about their most meaningful Christmas, they'll tell about the time a group of friends came through for them and became the body of Christ for them.

The group's ministry continued beyond Christmas. We didn't do all that we could have. We didn't do enough to take away the pain of losing little Kevin. But we did remember to send cards and to call on Kevin's birthday and the anniversary of his death. We couldn't take away Don and Sharon's grief, but we could make sure that they didn't grieve alone.

> *Do you know what's really sad? Every year at Christmastime there are couples who lost a child that year, yet no one notices or acknowledges that Christmas is going to be hell for them.*

Do you know what's really sad? Every year at Christmastime there are couples who lost a child that year, yet no one notices or acknowledges that Christmas is going to be hell for them. What is sad is that people have to grieve the passing of their parents alone. What's sad is that parents have children whom they've not heard from in months or years, and no one ever notices or asks or prays or cares. All around us, in every city in the world, people grieve alone. I have written this book to ask you to do something about it.

You see, we can't do anything about the fact that five-year-old boys have epilepsy. We can't do anything about the fact that moms spend Mother's Day in the hospital with their kids. Sharon wasn't the only mom in the hospital with her child that Mother's Day. We can't do anything about the fact that life can be excruciatingly painful at times. What we can do is to make sure that people don't have to go through those times alone. God never meant for us to go through the hard times alone. He gave us each other, and he commanded us to love.

In practical terms, this means giving Friday nights to Jesus, spending time on the telephone, and planning Valentine's Day dinners and Memorial Day picnics. We do all this during the normal times of life so we have bonds of friendship that will see us through the dark times.

I spent countless hours preparing this book so that I could ask you to do one thing. I want to ask you to rededicate the whole of your life to Christ and to his body. I want to invite you to take ownership of your part of the ministry so that the body of Christ functions as it should. It is all about relationships. I want to ask you to dedicate yourself to the cause of being a part of an army of believers that is advancing against the forces of darkness with the weapon of love. I want to ask you to give your time and attention to people inside and outside the body of Christ.

That's what it's all about. The church is not about quotas or programs or goals or procedures. It's about life. It's about spending time together, loving one another, laughing with each other, and, yes, facing death together.

I ask you to give yourself to reproducing your group every two years or less because God deserves to be worshiped by all people. I ask you to give yourself to doubling your class every two years or less because there are people who need to be loved. I ask you to use your gifts to grow your group because life can be terribly hard. I ask you to join me in this vision for the sheer thrill of following God in something bigger than all of us.

Would you take a moment right now and rededicate yourself to the calling of making a difference in this world through your small group? I am bowing my head even now to pray that you do. May God bless you richly as you represent him in a world that so desperately needs his love.